WHSMITH
HOME
AQUARIUM
IN COLOUR

WHSMITH HOME AQUARIUM
IN COLOUR

GWYNNE VEVERS

this edition produced exclusively for

WHSMITH

© Ward Lock Limited 1978

Produced specially for W. H. Smith & Sons
by Ward Lock Limited, 116 Baker Street,
London W1M 2BB, a member of the Pentos Group

Designed by Mel Saunders

Phototypeset in Monophoto Plantin
by Computer Photoset Ltd, Birmingham
Printed and bound in Singapore
by Toppan Printing Co

ISBN 0-7063-4184-8

Page one: *Apistogramma ramirezi*

Page three: *Herotilapia multispinosa*

Contents

Veiltail goldfish, different varieties

Introduction

For thousands of years man's interest in the waters of the world has been largely concerned with the exploitation of fishes and other aquatic animals as a source of food. The greater part of this harvest is obtained by hunting, using nets, trawls, traps and other devices. It is only in a few places that attempts have been made to farm fishes, but there is no doubt that this activity will increase significantly in the future.

The practice of keeping fishes in captivity is not new. The Chinese have been doing this for at least 2,000 years, mainly with goldfish and have produced a great array of shapes and colours in this particular fish. In Europe, a few fish species were kept in ponds by monks during the Middle Ages and used as a valuable source of animal protein. The maintenance of fishes for pleasure is, however, a very recent development in the western world. Evidently a few exotic species were starting to arrive in Europe during the 17th century, for Samuel Pepys has recorded an instance in his diary. It is really only in the last hundred years that tropical fishes have been transported to Europe, North America and elsewhere in significant numbers, and only in very recent years that these have travelled by air. It is now possible, for instance, for a consignment of fishes from Singapore to reach London in about thirty-six hours.

Most of the tropical aquarium fishes kept in captivity come from south-east Asia, Africa and central and southern America. The conditions in their home ranges are very variable. Some of the rivers and lakes in which they live have water which is rich in minerals, whereas others come from areas with soft water. The Amazon basin of South America is noted for the softness of its waters, but many of the lakes of central Africa have very hard, alkaline waters. Some natural waters are fast-flowing, others are almost stagnant, and there are also differences in temperature.

Fishes from such different environments will naturally require different conditions when they are kept in captivity. The methods used today for the maintenance of tropical fishes in aquarium tanks are the result of years of patient study and observation by aquarists, the vast majority of whom are essentially amateurs earning their living in other fields.

It is never possible to simulate natural conditions completely within the confines of an aquarium tank, but it is possible with modern techniques to produce very satisfactory conditions. In fact, it is no exaggeration to say that environmental conditions can be controlled far more efficiently in an aquarium tank than they can in a cage containing pandas, rats, birds or snakes. Many modern aquarists have a basic interest in the techniques of fish-keeping in addition to the aesthetic pleasure derived from the fishes themselves. In addition, they have a great ambition to breed their fishes, and in many cases they succeed.

The present book is intended to provide information on the basic principles of aquarium management, and to present in words and pictures a good selection of the many fishes, both freshwater and marine, which are available on the market and suitable for keeping in captivity. In addition, an account is given of some of the very attractive invertebrates, such as sea-anemones, crustaceans, molluscs and sea-urchins which can be kept in the marine aquarium.

1 Tanks and equipment

In general, the length of an aquarium tank should be greater than its height, and it should be so constructed that only one side is transparent. The back wall should be used for decorative rockwork. For a normal tank the ratio of length: width: height should be 10:5:6 or 10:3:4.

The number of fishes that can be put into a tank is usually given as the volume of water (in litres) required for each specimen. At one time it was said that each fish up to 5 cm (2 in) in length required a volume of 2 litres ($3\frac{1}{2}$ pints) of water, but this is certainly not enough. Beginners often lose sight of the fact that their fishes will grow if the conditions are suitable. It is much better to buy young fish and allow them to grow on in your own tank. Allow 2 litres ($3\frac{1}{2}$ pints) of water for each centimetre ($\frac{1}{3}$ in) of fish, provided the maximum height of the fish does not exceed 2 cm ($\frac{3}{4}$ in).

Thus, a tank measuring $80 \times 26 \times 38$ cm (approximately $32 \times 10 \times 15$ in) has a capacity of 79 litres (17 gallons), from which 14 litres (3 gallons) should be subtracted to allow for the volume of the decorative material, thus leaving 65 litres (14 gallons). If the aquarist intends to buy young neon tetras each 2cm ($\frac{3}{4}$in) long, then each one would require 4 litres (0·9 gallon) and the tank could be stocked with 65 divided by 4 = 16 fishes. This, however, is not recommended, because after a few months the fishes will have reached their maximum length of 4 cm ($1\frac{1}{2}$ in), so each would then require 8 litres (1·8 gallons) and the tank would be overcrowded. It would be better to start with not more than 10 to 12 fishes to allow for growth, and also for a few deaths.

Life in an aquarium tank is not static, for changes are taking place continually. The processes of growth and death will alter the general appearance of the tank, but these are natural phenomena and should result in a well-established tank with healthy inmates.

An angle-iron tank in anodized aluminium

Tanks constructed of welded angle-iron, with a bottom of metal or wired glass and panes of glass held in with mastic are gradually giving way to tanks with frames made of anodized aluminium with the glass panes bonded with silicone rubber. There are also tanks which have metal framing along the upper and lower edges only, the vertical joints being sealed with a silicone glue, an excellent material for aquarium purposes.

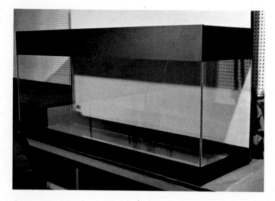

A tank with the panes sealed with silicone glue

Tanks can also be made of glass panes sealed with silicone glue alone, but here the glass itself must be somewhat thicker. The durability of the final product will depend on the quality of the materials used, as well as on the care with which they have been assembled. It is worth mentioning that silicone glues are not all the same. The hardening system is important for the final strength of the job, but the nature of the original solvent is important. Some use chemicals, such as phenol, which may release toxic substances, but it is quite safe to use a silicone-rubber glue in which the solvent is acetic acid, immediately recognizable because it smells of vinegar. Bostik 1581 Silicone Sealant has never caused any problems. Before using a silicone glue it is essential to ensure that the glass is completely free of grease or oil. Most glues harden with heat, but the hardening of silicone glues depends upon humidity, and the process takes about twenty-four hours.

Plastic tanks are attractive in appearance. The material can be bent and jointed, and a tank made from it is just as durable as any other. For aquarium purposes plastic is, in fact, just as good as glass and it does not scratch unless roughly handled.

Asbestos-cement tanks have become popular in recent years partly because they cannot corrode, which is an important point when sea water is being used. These tanks are heavy and have only one glass pane. Rockwork can be attached to the rear wall. The asbestos-cement sheets can be cut with a saw, but it is more convenient to buy the sheets ready cut from a dealer. The material may give off undesirable substances into the aquarium water, so all internal surfaces must be sealed by an epoxy resin, of the type sold as two components which are mixed immediately before use. The resin hardens very rapidly. If the tank is absolutely dry before the resin is applied, the result should be extremely durable.

The larger an aquarium tank the greater its weight, so one has to find out the weight of the tank when full, and relate this to the structure and strength of the flooring. A tank measuring $80 \times 26 \times 30$ cm (approximately $32 \times 10 \times 15$ in) holds about 80 litres (approximately 18 gallons) of water and this weighs 80 kg (176 lb). To this one must add the weight of the tank when empty, and that of its stand. If, however, the length of the tank is increased by only 20 cm (8 in), and the other dimensions in proportion, giving a tank measuring $100 \times 40 \times 50$ cm ($40 \times 16 \times 20$ in) then the capacity will be 200 litres (44 gallons), weighing 200 kg (440 lb). This is an increase in weight of over 150%, and of course the weight of the empty tank will also have increased.

It is best to place the tank in a dark corner of the room and to use lighting which can be properly controlled. Aquarium plants and fishes are adapted to living in tropical sunlight, and so the tank requires to be lit for the whole of the day if all the natural biological processes are to proceed as they should.

An aquarium tank should only be constructed by those with a practical bent who are used to working to exact standards, as faulty construction may have serious consequences. Normally proportioned tanks, such as those discussed above, can be obtained from aquarium dealers.

Many aquarists are concerned with the optical clarity of the water, but small amounts of visible detritus are not necessarily deleterious, whereas small amounts of invisible dissolved substances may cause trouble. Impurities in the water come from the faeces of the fishes and from the unconsumed remains of their food.

Aquarium water is undergoing changes the whole time. It has, for example, to be warmed, usually to 24-28°C (75-79°F), for the successful maintenance of tropical aquarium fishes. This increases the rate of evaporation of the water, but the mineral substances dissolved in it do not evaporate but remain in the tank water. If the tank is then topped up with ordinary fresh water this will add more dissolved material. In this way the water becomes increasingly 'dense' as the introduced substances become more concentrated. As the calcium becomes more concentrated the water becomes harder. A hardness testing kit will show how rapidly this happens.

Warm water evaporates more rapidly than cold, so the heating unit should never be set higher than is necessary. It is an advantage to fill the tank with water that is poor in mineral salts, perhaps with de-ionized water. This applies particularly in areas with hard mains water. If this method proves too expensive, it is possible to replace part of the water. This is better for the animals and plants than a renewal of all the water.

At one time aquarists dreamt and talked about the possibility of achieving a perfect natural equilibrium between animals, plants and water, but this almost never happens. It would need a very large tank with masses of plants and rather few fishes, and this would scarcely suit the modern aquarist.

Tank water can, however, be kept in good condition by various means, one of which is filtration. There are two principal types of filter: the internal and the external, which may be either fast or slow.

Internal filters are set up inside the aquarium tank and are therefore visible. The slow internal filter is a transparent plastic container filled with suitable medium, fixed in a corner of the tank, and fitted with an air-lift. With this type of filter, however, all the detritus in the water gets sucked in, so that the filter medium becomes clogged.

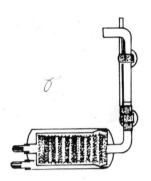

Internal filter with renewable cartridge

An internal filter with a cartridge is perhaps more efficient; this can be attached to the glass by suckers and is worked by an air-lift. When this becomes clogged the foam plastic cartridge can be renewed (see figure above).

In an ordinary tank the substrate does not have a constant flow of water passing through and so it does not receive oxygen. If the bottom is used as a filter then oxygen will reach it and beneficial aerobic bacteria can settle there. A substrate that is deficient in oxygen, on the other hand, will only have anaerobic bacteria, which produce metabolic products that foul the water and poison the fishes and plants. On the other hand, aerobic bacteria living in the substrate fulfil a useful purpose, for they convert waste products into substances that are biologically harmless.

Two systems of substrate filtration may be mentioned: one involves the slow flow of water from below upwards, the other having a rapid flow from above downwards. In the first method the connecting inlet tube (left in figure, page 12 top) leads to a shallow box on the bottom which has numerous slits. Water is pushed by an external motor down through the connecting tube and is distributed around the substrate which lies above the box. In this way the

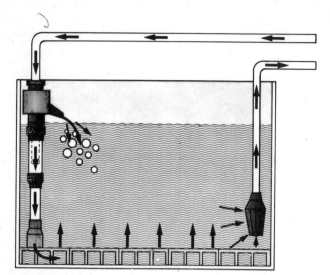

Substrate filtration with the water moving upwards through the substrate

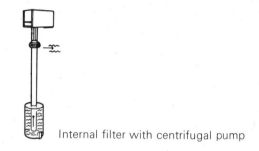

Internal filter with centrifugal pump

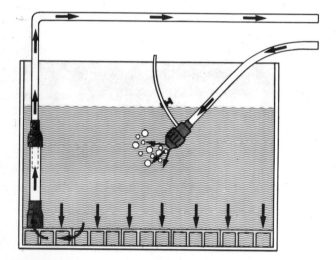

Substrate filtration with the water moving downwards through the substrate

substrate acts as a filter. The substrate itself must not of course be too fine or it will become clogged.

For rapid filtration flowing from above downwards, the connecting tube (on the left of figure, above) is connected with the suction end of the motor, and the tank water is sucked down through the substrate which again acts as a filter. The substrate must consist of coarse particles (5 mm ($\frac{1}{5}$ in) or more in diameter). This type of filtration is not suitable for a planted tank, but is excellent for keeping larger cichlids in tanks without plants.

Rapid filtration can also be carried out by

using a motor-driven internal filter with a centrifugal pump. This is used mainly for the marine aquarium, but it is also suitable for freshwater tanks, particularly those containing fish that dig (e.g. cichlids). These pumps produce rapid water movements, which suit fishes such as certain loaches, which come from fast-flowing rivers. The only disadvantage is that the rapid water movement soon brings detritus onto the filter medium, so that the container becomes clogged and no longer allows sufficient water to pass through. The pump will then stop unless the filter is cleaned.

External filters are much used for freshwater tanks. Not only are they efficient but they also have the advantage that all the technical equipment is out of sight.

External filter worked by an air-lift shown on the extreme right of lower diagram

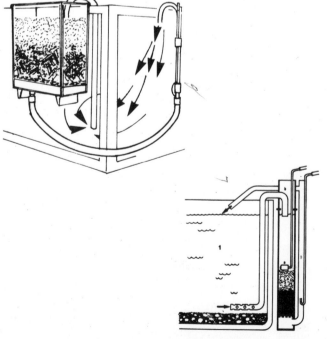

With a slow external filter the water is taken from the tank to the filter by an air-lift, which can move up to 200 litres (44 gallons) of water per hour. The external filter itself usually consists of a rectangular plastic container, open at the top, and filled with the filter medium. The water flows from the aquarium into the top of the filter, passes down through the filter medium, and is returned to the aquarium tank by an air-lift.

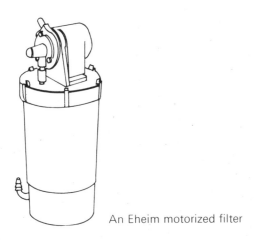

An Eheim motorized filter

The use of a motor-driven external filter provides faster filtration. The Eheim combined pumps and filters (figure, above) are designed for various tank sizes. Here the water is led into the filter from below and passes upwards through the medium with the help of the pump. This system is clean in operation and the filter medium, held in bags, is easily renewed.

The Eheim system is very efficient, but the filter medium must be changed at regular intervals. Some suggest that it should be changed every two weeks. If this is not done the water may appear to be relatively clean to the naked eye, but in practice the filter medium will have become clogged, and will be continually shedding impurities back into the aquarium water.

Various materials can be used for the filter, as for instance sand, gravel, nylon wool, activated charcoal, peat or certain new synthetic resins. Sand and gravel are very good, particularly when the two are used together, e.g. a com-

bination of coarse gravel/finer gravel/sand, which efficiently retains fine particles of detritus. Such a mixture is, however, heavy and difficult to handle, so nylon wool is usually used for catching some of the particles. This material is light in weight and extremely easy to clean. Glass wool should never be used in a filter, as tiny pieces break off and may injure or kill the fishes.

If activated charcoal is used for filtration the water should first be passed through a layer of nylon wool to remove the coarse particles of detritus. Activated charcoal has a structure of very fine pores which quickly become clogged by coarse particles. The nylon wool will only hold back a certain amount of waste material, so it must be cleaned regularly. Active charcoal will absorb only albuminous waste, but not ammonia in solution which is poisonous to fishes, nor the dissolved nitrites and nitrates that accumulate in aquarium water. If the charcoal is not renewed very frequently the filter will be removing visible waste but doing nothing else, and eventually albuminous substances absorbed by the charcoal will break down into ammonia and other poisonous substances.

Filtration through peat is also a very suitable method of treatment for most aquarium waters. It can have a most beneficial effect on life in the tank, but this will depend upon its quality, for not all peats are the same. One of the varying factors is the content of so-called humic acids, and this depends upon its place of origin. It is widely but erroneously believed that all peat is acid, but this is not so. 'Improved' horticultural peats enriched with fertilizers must not be used for aquarium purposes. Aquarist suppliers normally stock suitable acid peats. In addition to its content of humic acids and its ability to lower the pH of the water (acidification), peat also contains hormone-like substances, which are known, for example, to encourage the growth of young plants.

In a well-kept aquarium tank the correct numbers of beneficial bacteria do a continuous job of breaking down and converting organic waste materials. On the other hand, badly kept tanks, with an excess of waste matter, become breeding grounds for enormous numbers of injurious bacteria. This leads to clouding of the water, due to the multiplication of single-celled protozoans, which feed on the bacteria. This state of affairs is not good for either plants or fishes, and indeed some aquarium fishes, such as cardinal tetras and discus fishes, which are difficult to breed, are known to be particularly sensitive to the presence of bacteria. This problem can be largely solved by filtration through peat, which reduces the load of micro-organisms.

Peat soon loses its beneficial properties and must then be renewed, perhaps every three to four weeks, and a proportion of the water can be replaced at the same time.

The majority of aquarium fishes come from the tropics, and so their tank water must be heated. Most tropical waters have temperatures in the region of 22–26°C (72–79°F), rising sometimes to 30°C (86°F). These are the approximate temperatures at which aquarium water should be kept, although during the winter months (November to February) some tropical fishes can tolerate a drop of a few degrees.

A tropical aquarium should not be subject to sudden variations in temperature, and so it should never be installed in a place where this can occur, e.g. in a draughty corridor, or close to a radiator. A sudden drop in temperature has an inhibiting effect on metabolism and on the blood circulation, and it reduces resistance to disease. It may also affect the functioning of the swimbladder, and this results in abnormal swimming.

The electric heaters now used in aquarium tanks work on the same principle as an immersion heater. The wattage of the heater should be roughly the same as the volume of water to be heated, i.e. 100 watts for 100 litres (22 gallons).

There are two types of heater: the ordinary aquarium heater (figure b) which can be con-

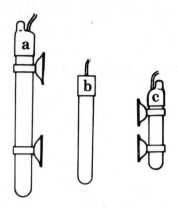

a) heater with thermostat
b) heater without thermostat
c) thermostat without the heater

trolled by a separate thermostat (figure c) and the combined heater and thermostat (figure a). The latter should be used for small tanks. For larger tanks (length over 100 cm or 40 in) it is better to install the necessary number of heaters, and to have these controlled by a single thermostat. The filter will help to keep the water moving so that the heat is dispersed. The operative part of the heater is a wire element wound round an insulated tube, which is sealed into an outer glass casing.

It is quite essential that the heater itself should not be buried in the substrate, nor touching the tank glass. Most types of heater can be fixed to the glass by suction cups. The thermostat is set at a given temperature, and being coupled to the heater it then keeps the water at this temperature.

There is thermostatically controlled switch equipment which is particularly useful for breeding, where a series of tanks of the same size each with its own heater can be controlled by a single thermostat.

Aeration is often valued rather too highly. In most cases it certainly helps to circulate the water, but it is not very efficient at increasing the oxygen content. In general, aeration is not so important in a freshwater tank as it is in a marine one, where the fishes, and particularly the invertebrates, need it.

In practice oxygen enters the water at its surface, and obviously the greater the surface area the more oxygen can be absorbed, assuming that the surface is clean. Occasionally a tank develops a thin surface layer of dust and oil and this prevents the interchange of gases (oxygen and carbon dioxide). This slightly iridescent layer is also dangerous to surface-living fishes, and it must be removed by drawing tissue paper across it.

The two main constituents of air are oxygen and nitrogen, and for aquarium purposes it is the oxygen which is of primary importance. Water absorbs oxygen more readily than nitrogen, so that the air dissolved in water is relatively richer in oxygen than atmospheric air. In addition, the oxygen content is higher in cool water, in moving waters and in waters rich in vegetation. Oxygen escapes rapidly from heated tank water. The rate of respiration of the fishes then increases as they attempt to get more oxygen, and eventually they come to the surface to gulp air. At the same time the fishes will be producing carbon dioxide, which will further worsen the situation. A proportion of the water can then be replaced with new water at the same temperature, or an aerator will effectively move the water round so that the surface changes the whole time and oxygen enters. This is the main function of aeration, for not much of the oxygen in the air bubbles is actually released into the water.

One of the simplest methods of aeration is to use a small diaphragm pump, which propels air through a length of tubing and releases it into

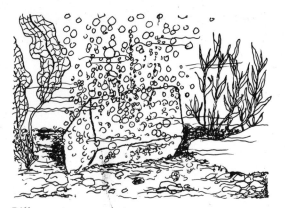

Diffuser stone, or airstone

the water as a stream of bubbles. By using a diffuser stone the bubbles will be much finer.

The disadvantage of this method is that bubbles of air are released in large numbers, and most rise directly to the surface and produce a spray, which settles on the tank cover and lamps. In a marine tank the water part of the spray will evaporate, leaving a crust consisting of a mixture of salts, and this builds up quite rapidly. Even in a freshwater tank the spray will contain some calcium and this will appear as an opaque greyish film.

An alternative method is to use a diaphragm pump to operate an air-lift. The principle is quite simple. A glass or rigid plastic tube is positioned vertically in the water so that its bottom end is about an inch above the substrate, while its top end protrudes about an inch or so above the water surface and is bent over at an angle. Air from the pump is led into the bottom of the tube and as the bubbles rise they carry water with them, so that a mixture of air and water reaches the top where it is expelled. This mixture can either fall back into the aquarium tank directly or it can fall onto an external filter. In either case the water will have been enriched with oxygen.

If the pump has to be switched off for some reason, there is always a chance that as the pump pressure drops water will be sucked back up the delivery tube and possibly into the pump itself, and this will obviously cause damage. To prevent this happening it is best to position the pump well above the tank.

Diagram showing the structure of a diaphragm pump

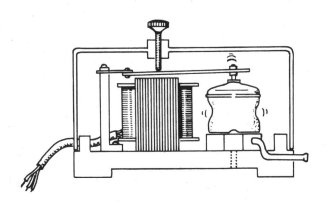

The light requirements of fishes and water plants vary considerably, and in the wild there are of course daily and seasonal fluctuations in light. Some plants and fishes like plenty of sunlight, others need less. Strong sunlight over a prolonged period may cause the plants to produce so much oxygen that the water becomes saturated. Under such conditions the fishes will suffer.

In nature, fishes and other aquatic organisms always receive light from above. In a home aquarium, on the other hand, light can enter from all four sides as well as from above. It is therefore not advisable to position the tank close to a window which may from time to time receive bright sunlight. It is much better to have the aquarium elsewhere in the room, possibly in a dark corner, and to illuminate it with artificial lighting which is controllable. Thus an aquarium tank becomes independent of the seasonal changes of light found in temperate regions.

The introduction of fluorescent lighting solved the problem of finding a bright light source in a shallow fitting. In choosing the best type of fluorescent lamp the requirements of the aquarium plants are of primary importance. The assimilation process of plants, or photosynthesis, is mainly dependent upon the blue and the red parts of the spectrum. Special fluorescent tubes have been developed which produce this type of light, e.g. Osram Fluora and Sylvania Gro-lux. The mixture of red and blue rays emitted by these lamps stimulates plant growth.

Aquarium lighting encourages plant growth and enhances the colours of the fishes. The suggestions given in the table (below) are intended to act as guide-lines.

By installing switch equipment it is possible to switch each lamp on and off at will, and thus to vary the amount of light. It is possible to have too much light, and this may lead to excessive growth of algae. A small amount of green algae on the rocks is quite normal and it supplies extra food for some fishes, and for snails. On the other hand, brown or beige-coloured algae will grow if the light is too weak; and excessive growth of green algae or the appearance of blue-green algae suggests that the light is too strong. It is then usually sufficient to switch off one lamp.

Aquarium lighting

Tank size length × width × height in cm (inches in brackets)	Capacity in litres (gallons in brackets)	No.	Fluorescent tubes required
60 × 25 × 40 (approximately 24 × 10 × 16)	60 (13)	1	20W Gro-lux (in front of tank)
		1	20W Universal White
80 × 40 × 50 (approximately 32 × 16 × 20)	160 (35)	1	20W Gro-lux (in front)
		1	20W Universal white
		1	20W Warm tone de luxe
100 × 40 × 50 (approximately 40 × 16 × 20)	200 (44)	1	20W Gro-lux
		1	25W Universal white
		1	25W Warm tone de luxe
130 × 50 × 50 (approximately 52 × 20 × 20)	325 (71½)	1	40W Gro-lux (in front)
		1	20W Warm tone de luxe
		1	40W Universal white

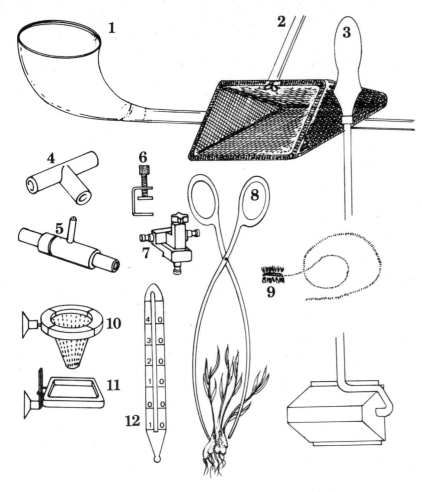

Various aquarium accessories:
1) glass pipe for catching fry
2) capture net
3) glass cleaner with blade
4) T-piece for tubing
5) Eheim diffuser for 10 mm ($\frac{2}{5}$ in) tubing
6) tubing clip
7) tap controlling three outlets
8) tongs for moving plants
9) brush for cleaning tubing
10) sieve for feeding *Tubifex* worms to fish
11) feeding ring for dry food
12) thermometer, reading up to 40°C (104°F)

In the tropics the maximum length of daylight is sixteen hours. So it is probably best to fit an electric time clock into the circuit so that the lighting comes on at the proper time and the fishes receive the amount of light and darkness they would in the wild. For many fishes the arrival of dawn (or the switching on of the aquarium lighting), acts as a signal. Some, for instance, spawn at this time of day. Similarly at twilight many species look for a suitable place to spend the night, and in those that protect their brood, one can observe the parent fishes gathering the young into a hole or pit, or in the case of mouthbrooding cichlids into the parent's mouth.

All technical equipment must be kept in full working order, to avoid loss of money and, more particularly, of valuable fishes. Repairs to equipment often take several weeks, but fortunately aquarium dealers stock spare parts for the main items of equipment.

Other items that will be needed include nets of various sizes for catching fishes, an aquarium scraper for cleaning the glass, a pair of forceps or tongs for picking up plants, and a thermometer for checking the temperature of the water. Plastic taps can be used for adjusting the flow of air from a diaphragm pump, or it is simpler to fit a tubing clamp of the type used in chemical laboratories. A long, thin brush is useful for cleaning the plastic tubing connecting the tank and the filter.

2 Setting up the aquarium

The material used to cover the bottom of an aquarium is generally known as the substrate. Suitable materials include coarse river sand with a particle diameter of 1·5mm (approximately $\frac{1}{16}$in) and gravel (diameter 3–4mm, approximately $\frac{1}{8}$in), both of which are sold by aquarium dealers. Finer sand packs too closely so that the water in it tends to stagnate. Movement of water through the substrate is essential for the maintenance of the micro-organisms responsible for the breakdown of various waste products.

The substrate may contain the eggs of snails or other unwelcome organisms. These can be destroyed by putting the sand or gravel into a large plastic container filled with water to which potassium permanganate is added to give a dark red colour. This should be thoroughly stirred and left to stand for two days. The liquid is then poured off and the sand or gravel washed several times in fresh water.

The substrate is primarily intended for the plants, but in fact most water plants take in their nutrients in dissolved form directly from the

The substrate of an aquarium should be clean, decorative and functional

water, through the whole of the submerged surface. On the other hand, marsh plants, such as *Cryptocoryne,* obtain their nutrients mainly through the roots.

True water plants use the substrate primarily for anchorage. To compensate for certain deficiencies the water can from time to time be enriched with special liquid fertilizer, obtainable on the market.

Some fishes and plants require extremely soft water, and for these it is quite essential that the substrate is free from any snail or other mollusc shells, as these contain calcium, which will soon increase the hardness of the water.

All decorative rocks must be thoroughly scrubbed with a brush and washed under running water. Pieces of igneous rock, such as granite, gneiss, quartz and basalt are ideal for this purpose, but sedimentary rocks such as limestone, marble and sandstone ought not to be used when the water has to be kept soft, as they will increase its hardness. To test whether a rock contains calcium, just put a few drops of hydrochloric or sulphuric acid onto it. If it effervesces the rock contains calcium and should not be used in soft water.

Flat rocks are good for tank decoration as they can be arranged to form caves of various sizes, which provide hiding-places for the fishes. In tanks for large cichlids, which dig vigorously, the rockwork must be very firmly constructed to prevent it being undermined and collapsing. If a small amount of cement is used it should be sealed, when thoroughly dry, with an epoxy resin. If this is not done the cement may release toxic substances into the water.

For dwarf cichlids, which are rather more sensitive than their larger relatives, many aquarists use peat blocks. These can be cut to provide caves and tunnels, but they need a good soaking to remove the air.

Well-washed tree roots can also be used. They should not just lie on the substrate but should be raised up above it so that the space beneath them can provide shelter for the fishes. Most fishes, particularly when at rest, try to hide so that they cannot be seen from the water surface. In among the rocks and roots there can be small groups of aquatic plants, some of which can be species that grow up and have broad leaves that float at the surface.

After the vegetation has been planted, a layer of rounded basalt chips can be spread over the substrate. This makes it darker. Peat can also be used but this is not done so much nowadays, except when keeping egg-laying toothcarps. In such cases a layer of peat 1–2 cm ($\frac{1}{3}$–$\frac{3}{4}$ in) thick would be appropriate but this will, of course, need to be renewed from time to time.

As with all aquarium materials, it is quite essential that any new or unknown plastic should be tested, in order to ensure that it is not releasing toxic substances into the water. Silicone rubber can safely be used as a form of glue, and it sets under the influence of humidity. On the other hand, many household glues require a certain amount of warmth for hardening. Epoxy resins form an excellent hard coating for aquarium purposes, but they must only be applied to absolutely dry objects. When liquid these resins give off toxic fumes, so they should be used only in properly ventilated areas.

Fresh waters vary considerably in composition, depending largely upon their origin. With the exception of distilled water, which is an artificial product, all waters contain some dissolved matter which they acquire as they pass through different soils and rocks.

Unlike sea water, which is very uniform in composition, the waters of rivers and lakes are much influenced by the structure of the surrounding country, e.g. marshland, limestone uplands or estuaries. Sea water contains large amounts of minerals, originally derived from soils and rock, and is very hard. This is not so in most rivers. The Rio Negro in South America, for instance, has extremely soft water, poor in minerals, for it flows through areas where calcium is almost completely lacking. This dark brown water contains large amounts of humic acids, derived from flooded marshland, leaves and rotting timber, and it has an acid pH. Fishes from such waters are often difficult to keep, and particularly to breed, in ordinary tap water, much of which is hard.

The two types of water hardness, namely carbonate hardness and non-carbonate hardness, together make up the total hardness. For the aquarist the most convenient method of measuring hardness is the German system, in which one degree of hardness (1° DH) is the equivalent of 10 milligrams of calcium oxide dissolved in 1 litre of water. British and American degrees of hardness are expressed as parts per million of calcium carbonate, 1 British or US degree being 14·3 parts per million of calcium carbonate. Conversion of these two systems is quite easy:

$$\text{British or US degrees} = \text{DH} \times \frac{56}{100}$$

German degrees

$$= \text{British or US degrees} \times \frac{100}{56}$$

Water hardness is often of decisive importance when keeping certain fish species. Carbonate or temporary hardness, due to the presence of calcium carbonate, can be removed by boiling. Non-carbonate or permanent hardness is due to the presence of various compounds, mainly calcium sulphate and certain salts of magnesium. This type of hardness can be removed only by chemical means (e.g. sodium phosphate, Permutit). The following table is intended as a guide to hardness, distilled water having 0° DH:

Very soft water	= 0–4° DH
Soft water	= 5–8° DH
Medium-hard water	= 8–12° DH
Fairly hard water	= 13–18° DH
Hard water	= 19–30° DH
Very hard water	= over 30° DH

The hardness of the water used in some towns and cities may fluctuate. It is therefore advisable to test the hardness of mains water from time to time.

If the mains water is much too hard it can be modified by the addition of distilled water, although this may be quite expensive. The amount of distilled water required can be calculated if one knows the hardness of the mains water and the type of water required. If, for example, the mains water is 16° DH and distilled water is 0° DH and the aquarist wants a water with a hardness of 2° DH, then:

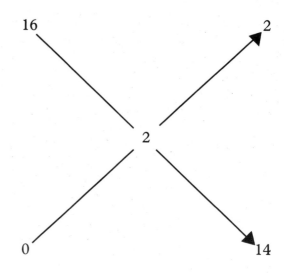

This diagram shows that fourteen parts of distilled water must be mixed with two parts of mains water to give a water with a hardness of 2° DH.

Temporary hardness removed by boiling will very slowly return as the water takes up carbon dioxide, so that bicarbonate is formed.

More rarely, the aquarist may have water that is too soft for his purpose. For example, many of the cichlids from African lakes require hard water. This can be obtained by adding a small amount of a solution of pure calcium sulphate, until the desired hardness is obtained.

The letters pH stand for pondus Hydrogenii or the weight of hydrogen. Water consists of H_2O molecules, dissociated into positively charged hydrogen ions (H^+) and negatively charged hydroxyl ions (HO^-). In neutral or distilled water the number of H and HO ions is the same, and the H ions in a litre of water weigh 10^{-7} grams or 0·0000001 grams, while the HO ions weigh the same. This figure is known as the pH value of the water. For convenience only the logarithm of the hydrogen value is written, omitting the negative sign. Thus the pH value of neutral water is 7, written as pH7. The pH of rain and melted snow is also 7. In acid water the pH value is less than 7, in alkaline it is greater. Waters of the temperate zone are mostly slightly alkaline with pH values between 7·5 and 9, but most tropical waters have pH values between 5 and 6·8, and are therefore acid to slightly acid. The exceptions include the waters of the central African lakes. Lake Tanganyika has water of about pH 8·8, and Lake Malawi about pH 8·0. Further to the north Lake Rudolf, which is poor in fish, has a pH between 9·5 and 10·0. Even the soda lakes of East Africa (e.g. Lake Magadi), with a pH of about 11·5, still have some fishes (e.g. *Tilapia grahami*).

Special kits for measuring the pH can be bought. When the water is already very soft it can be acidified by adding a peat extract or preferably by filtering the tank water through peat. A peat filter should be renewed every two weeks. Aquarium waters treated with peat are particularly suitable for species of *Nannostomus*, *Aphyosemion* and *Symphysodon* as well as neon tetras and harlequin fishes.

Many labyrinth fishes, rasboras and various species of *Hyphessobrycon* prefer a pH between 6 and 7, whereas most barbs, some catfishes (e.g. *Otocinclus*) and African cichlids (e.g. *Hemichromis*) only do well when the pH is 7·0–8·5. There are relatively few fishes which require a pH between 5 and 6, and a water hardness of 3–6° DH. These include the characins *Paracheirodon innesi, Cheirodon axelrodi, Hyphessobrycon heterorhabdus, Nannostomus trifasciatus* and *Micralestes interruptus*, the rasboras *Rasbora heteromorpha* and *R. maculatus*, the species of *Aphyosemion* and other egg-laying toothcarps, and the cichlids *Symphysodon discus, S. aequifasciata* and some species of *Apistogramma*.

In contrast, there are some fishes, such as the mollies of the genus *Poecilia*, which require slightly brackish water, so they should be kept in water containing 1 heaped tablespoon or 30 grams of sea salt per litre ($1\frac{3}{4}$ pints). The salt should be dissolved in a small quantity of warm water, and added gradually to the tank, with constant stirring.

In the tropics a certain amount of lake and river water evaporates the whole time, but this is replaced by rain. In the aquarium, water lost by evaporation should be replaced by soft water, because the percentage of dissolved salts will increase as water evaporates.

In the tropical areas from which most aquarium fishes come the water is usually very soft, and poor in dissolved minerals. Some waters in the Amazon basin may, for instance, have a pH value as low as 4·5–4·9. Yet in the wild, fishes such as the cardinal tetra *(Cheirodon axelrodi)* live in this water. Fishes that come from such waters poor in mineral salts (soft waters) need to have the same type of water for breeding, even though as adults they may have been acclimatized in the aquarium to living in a harder, mineral-rich water.

3 Freshwater aquarium plants

Aquarium plants are often regarded purely in terms of decoration, but this is not the whole story. Aquatic plants and fishes use oxygen for respiration and release carbon dioxide. During the day fishes take up oxygen and release carbon dioxide, which is used by green plants in the process of assimilation, in which the plants, possessing the green pigment chlorophyll, take in water and mineral salts, and by using the sun's energy are able to build up organic substances, such as sugars. Animals cannot do this, the ability to do so being restricted to green plants. During assimilation in daylight, the plants release excess oxygen which the fishes use for respiration. Thus there is a state of biological equilibrium (see below).

At night the plants cease to assimilate, but take up some oxygen and release excess carbon dioxide. However, the small amount of oxygen they remove does not affect the resting fishes. In general, an aquarium tank has its lowest oxygen content and its highest carbon dioxide content in the morning, but normally this is not dangerous.

The amount of oxygen released into the water by the plants depends upon the total surface area of the leaves. The larger the area the greater the amount of oxygen produced. In plants with large, flat leaves the total surface area is proportionately less than it is in those with numerous, fine feathery leaflets, e.g. *Cabomba, Myriophyllum, Elodea* and Java moss

(Vesicularia). Plants that require much light and grow rapidly should be put in those parts of the tank that receive most light. Such plants will tend to overshadow smaller ones, but these are often plants which do not need so much light. Delicate, feathery plants almost always need a lot of light, and they do not tolerate algae growing on them.

Unlike land plants, many of those that live in the water are able to take up mineral salts through their general surface as well as through the roots, thus acquiring dissolved substances, which they use in building up their tissues.

In a well-established tank faeces and decaying leaves form detritus on the bottom and this will be broken down by micro-organisms in the substrate into substances that are then taken up by the plants. Excess detritus is almost always a sign that the tank contains too many fishes, so that the biological equilibrium has been upset.

Some fishes, such as the anabantids, thrive in an aquarium with dense vegetation, but fishes from open waters like space for swimming, so planting should be restricted to a few scattered groups along the side and rear walls.

Some fishes use feathery plants as a spawning site. Labyrinth fishes will often make their bubble nests close to floating plants, while others like the half shade produced by such plants. Angelfishes tend to bite and tear broad leaves, so their tank should have tough plants such as *Vallisneria, Sagittaria* and Amazon sword plants *(Echinodorus)*. Cichlids are often difficult to keep together with plants because they dig so vigorously, and here it is best to put the plants in small flowerpots and anchor them firmly in the bottom. Many fishes disturb the surface of the substrate, stirring up mud, which settles on the plants. This is particularly undesirable in the case of plants with feathery leaves.

Most aquarium plants like water that is soft, slightly acid and warm. Species of *Cryptocoryne*, which are really marsh plants, should be planted in water with a maximum depth of 30 cm (12 in), and if they do not appear to be doing well they probably need a somewhat softer water.

Aquarium plants should not be positioned at random. The individual species should be gathered in small groups, separated from one another by rockwork or roots. The individual plants in each group should not be planted too close together, as they will soon grow and spread. Two or three species would be sufficient for a small tank.

About once a year any plants that have grown too large can be removed, thus giving more light and space for the others, and all withered and damaged leaves must be removed.

Before planting, the tank must be thoroughly cleaned to remove filamentous algae, snail spawn and pockets of dirt, and then disinfected for about twenty minutes with a solution of potassium permanganate (enough to give a deep pink colour). An additional bath in hydrogen peroxide (1 teaspoonful to each litre (1¾ pints) of water) for five to ten minutes is also recommended. After the tank has been washed out with fresh water, the plants should be carefully rinsed and their roots slightly pruned, as this promotes growth. The tank is then filled with water to a depth of 10 cm (3¾ in).

The tallest plants should be put in at the back, close to the rear wall, while smaller species are planted in the foreground. The roots should be carefully covered with sand or gravel, gently firmed with the fingers, and the whole plant pulled upwards very gently, so that the top of the roots is just clear of the substrate. Each plant requires an area of about 5 sq cm (2 sq in), but the exact space will depend upon its rate of growth and final size. Plants that grow large, such as *Cryptocoryne griffithii, C. ciliata* or *C. beckettii* should be planted at least 15 cm (6 in) apart.

Aquatic plants that take in water and minerals through their general surface can be planted as rootless cuttings, after removal of the lower two or three leaves, and anchored by stones until they have rooted.

Aquatic plants that derive their nutrients from the substrate by means of their roots include *Aponogeton, Echinodorus* and *Cryptocoryne*. These can be planted in shallow flowerpots in a mixture of two-thirds loam and aquarium peat to one-third of the substrate being used in the rest of the tank. This method allows the plants to be removed without damaging their roots when the substrate is being cleaned. The best time for planting is spring, when young plants have finished their resting period (November to January) and are beginning to grow rapidly.

Aquarium plants are mostly propagated by vegetative means, that is, by cuttings, runners and division of plants or roots, which should be done in spring. Runners should not be separated from the parent plant until they have formed proper roots. Cuttings are obtained by taking branches or by pruning back a main stem.

Aquarium plants can be divided into groups depending on their leaf form. Thus:
Group 1.
Plants with strap-like leaves, which mostly acquire nutrients through the roots. They produce plenty of oxygen.
Group 2.
Plants with coarse or mossy leaves, which acquire nutrients through the general surface. They often act as spawning sites.
Group 3.
Long-stalked plants requiring subdued light and soft water.

Group 4.
Plants with feathery leaves, acquiring nutrients through the surface, some requiring soft water and good light.

Group 5.
Floating plants requiring bright light and air, so the tank should be uncovered. Often used by fishes for spawning.

Group 6.
Rooted plants with floating leaves, requiring good overhead lighting. Some are best grown in pots.

Group 7.
Marsh plants, many of which grow well, if slowly, when totally submerged.

In the following notes the group is indicated by the bracketed figure printed after the scientific name.

Acorus gramineus, a grass-like plant

Acorus gramineus (1)
A grass-like plant with leaves up to 40 cm (16 in) long, which is good for a marsh aquarium, and does best in temperate water.

Anubias nana (3).
A marsh plant from the African tropical rain-forests, which likes soft water at a temperature of about 24°C (75°F) and good but not bright light. It does not do so well when the leaves are continuously submerged.

Aponogeton madagascariensis
(formerly *A. fenestralis*) (3)
This is the Madagascar lace-plant which is not at all easy to grow. It produces winter buds which require a resting period at a reduced temperature, and indeed will die if kept too warm.

Anubias nana, a marsh plant

Aponogeton madagascariensis, Madagascar lace plant

Aponogeton ulvaceus (3)

Another decorative plant from Madagascar, with pale yellow-green wavy leaves, that is not too difficult to grow in an uncrowded position in a large tank. Other species in the genus include *A. crispus*, *A. elongatus*, *A. natans* and *A. undulatus*.

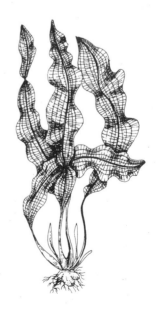

Aponogeton ulvaceus, a decorative plant with yellow-green wavy leaves

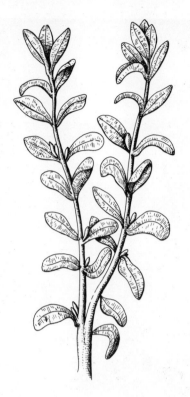

Bacopa monniera, a marsh plant

Bacopa monniera (2)

A marsh plant which can tolerate a wide range of temperatures (15–26°C or 59–79°F) and is best grown in a coarse sandy substrate, soft to medium-hard water and good light. Propagation is by cuttings. The large-leaved related species *B. amplexicaulis* is not so suitable for growing continually submerged.

Barclaya longifolia, a tropical rain forest plant

Barclaya longifolia (3).

A handsome plant from the tropical rain-forests of south-east Asia, requiring a substrate of loam and coarse sand, with very soft water at a temperature of 25–28°C (77–82°F), but really only suitable for the expert. Care should be taken to ensure that the substrate does not become too cold. It will quickly be eaten by snails.

Cabomba aquatica (4)

The genus *Cabomba* has a wide distribution extending from southern North America to Central and South America. The best species for the aquarium is *C. aquatica*, which requires very soft water and plenty of light. It is propagated by cuttings inserted in a mixture of loam and coarse sand, which are then placed in the tank at a water temperature of 20–28°C (68–82°F). Other species include *C. australis*, *C. caroliniana* and *C. piauhyensis*.

Ceratopteris cornuta, a floating water fern

Ceratopteris cornuta (5)

A floating water fern well suited for a tank with sufficient space between the water surface and the tank cover, or even better for an uncovered tank. The water should be soft to medium-hard, at a temperature of 20–30°C (68–86°F). A single plant may attain a diameter of about 50 cm (20 in). Daughter plantlets produced vegetatively can be used for propagation.

Cabomba, a plant with finely divided leaves

Ceratopteris thalictroides, Sumatra fern, broad-leaved form

Ceratopteris thalictroides, Sumatra fern, fine-leaved form

Ceratopteris thalictroides (3)

Also known as Sumatra fern, this species occurs in fine-leaved and broad-leaved forms. The plants should not be inserted too deep in the substrate. Propagation is by daughter plantlets.

Cryptocoryne affinis
(formerly *C. haerteliana*) (3)

The genus *Cryptocoryne* has a large number of marsh plants very widely grown in the aquarium. *C. affinis*, from Malaya, grows to a height of 15 cm (6 in). The uppersides of the leaves are dark blue-green, the undersides pale green (in subdued light) or wine-red (in bright light). They can be grown in a mixture of loam and peat covered with coarse sand, with a moderate amount of light, soft water and at a temperature of 22–26°C (72–79°F). *Cryptocoryne* species should be planted in groups and left to grow undisturbed.

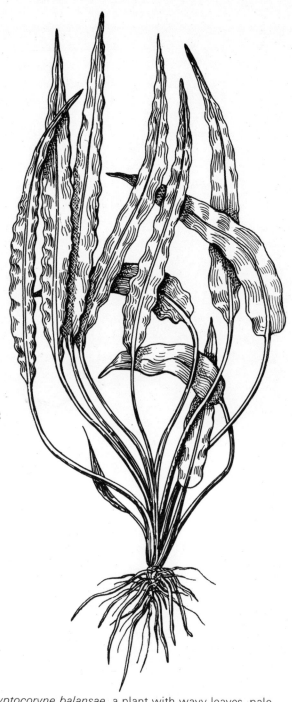

Cryptocoryne affinis, a plant from Malaya

Cryptocoryne balansae, a plant with wavy leaves, pale green on both sides

Cryptocoryne balansae
(formerly *C. somphongsii*) (3)

One of the larger species of *Cryptocoryne*, sometimes reaching a height of about 30 cm (12 in). It comes from Vietnam and Thailand. The wavy leaves are pale green on both sides. In general this species can be grown in the same way as *C. affinis*, but it can also be planted on its own, not in a group.

foreground of an aquarium tank, where it should spread quite quickly.

Cryptocoryne ciliata, a plant with bright green leaves

Cryptocoryne ciliata (3)

Widely distributed in south-east Asia, this species has bright green leaves and reaches a height of 40 cm (16 in), growing above the water surface if not prevented by the tank cover.

Cryptocoryne purpurea, a small very decorative plant

Cryptocoryne purpurea (3)

A small, very decorative Malayan species, scarcely reaching a height of 10 cm (3¾ in), and to be cultivated like *C. affinis.* The leaves are dark green on both sides, the undersides having a reddish tinge, becoming darker with age.

Cryptocoryne nevillii, a smaller plant of the Cryptocoryne genus

Cryptocoryne nevillii (3)

A smaller species, originally from Ceylon (Sri Lanka), and very suitable for planting in the

Cryptocoryne wendtii, a plant with leaves of dark green on the upper sides, pale red-tinged green on the undersides

Cryptocoryne wendtii (3)

A species from south-east Asia which usually grows rapidly to a height of 12 cm (4¾in). The uppersides of the leaves are dark, the undersides pale green with a reddish tinge. To be cultivated in the same way as *C. affinis*. Other species suitable for the aquarium include *C. beckettii, C. blassii, C. griffithii, C. longicauda, C. johorensis, C. versteegii* (from Papua-New Guinea and only 6 cm (2¼in) in height) and the very tall *C. retrospiralis*.

They grow rapidly in soft to medium-hard water. *E. amazonicus*, from Brazil, reaches a height of at least 30 cm (12 in) and is very suitable for cultivating by itself in a shallow pot with a mixture of loam and coarse sand. Propagation is by runners or plantlets that develop vegetatively.

Echinodorus bleheri, one of the larger plants of the Echinodorus genus

Echinodorus bleheri
(formerly *E. paniculatus*) (3)
One of the larger members of the genus, reaching a height of at least 40 cm (16 in) and cultivated in the same way as *E. amazonicus*.

Echinodorus amazonicus, a handsome plant

Echinodorus amazonicus
(formerly *E. brevipedicellatus*) (3)
Species of the genus *Echinodorus*, generally known as Amazon sword plants, have tough, robust leaves, which few fishes will try to eat.

Echinodorus cordifolius, a plant with heart-shaped leaves on long stems

Echinodorus latifolius, a small, rapidly-growing plant

Echinodorus cordifolius (3)

Originally from Central and South America and sometimes sold as *E. radicans*. The heart-shaped leaves on long stems grow to a height of about 20 cm (7¾ in) in soft water and plenty of light, but the temperature should not be too high.

Echinodorus latifolius
(formerly *E. magdalenensis*) (3)

An excellent aquarium plant from Colombia, growing to a height of 15 cm (6 in), which should be kept like the other species of *Echinodorus*, except that the water temperature can be much lower (up to about 16°C or 61°F).

Echinodorus tenellus, a charming small sword plant

Echinodorus tenellus (3)

A small sword plant from tropical and subtropical America, up to 8 cm (3 in) tall, which is particularly suitable for the foreground of a tank. It is sometimes erroneously sold as *Sagittaria microfolia*. It should be planted in a mixture of sand and gravel, but it is not always easy to keep. Propagation is by runners.

Other species suitable for the aquarium include *E. berteroi*, *E. martii*, *E. muricatus* and *E. nymphaeifolius*.

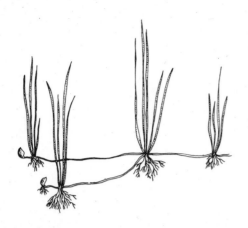

Eleocharis acicularis (3)
A small North American sedge for the fore-ground of a tank, with needle-shaped leaves that often reach a height of 20 cm (7¾ in). The water should be soft to medium-hard, at a temperature not exceeding 22°C (72°F).

Eleocharis acicularis, a small sedge plant

Elodea densa, a robust, fast-growing plant suitable for beginner aquarists

Elodea densa (2)

This is a good robust, fast-growing aquarium plant for the beginner, which will grow at temperatures between 12° and 28°C (54–82°F), and in subdued or bright light. The water can be medium-hard, and the cuttings can simply be inserted in the sand. The related species *E. canadensis* (Canadian waterweed) and *E. callitrichoides* (Chilean waterweed) are not suitable for tropical tanks as they do not tolerate temperatures above 18°C (64°F). *E. canadensis* is, however, suitable for a cold-water tank.

Hydrocleis nymphoides, a very handsome plant, but not very suitable for the standard aquarium

Hydrocleis nymphoides (1)

A handsome American plant for the specialist, but not really suitable for the standard aquarium, as it requires a tank with a large surface area in a well-lit, airy position and does not

tolerate condensation water dripping on it. It can be cultivated in a mixture of rich loam and sand in water at a temperature of 22–28°C (72–82°F), but the tank must be tall as the floating leaves grow to a length of 25 cm (10 in).

Hygrophyla difformis, a plant from south-east Asia

Hygrophila difformis
(formerly *Synnema triflorum*) (4)

A plant from south-east Asia, somewhat resembling *Ceratopteris* but with larger, more compact leaves, and growing to a height of about 50 cm (20 in). It should be cultivated in bright light and soft water at a temperature of 22–28°C (72–82°F), and propagated by cuttings.

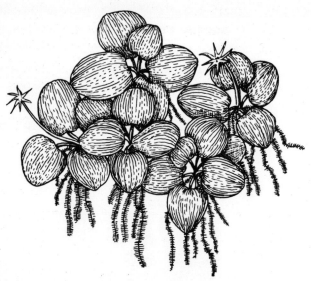

Limnobium stoloniferum, a small floating plant

It should be cultivated in soft water and under bright light. Propagation is by cuttings inserted into a mixture of sand and loam, but the cut ends give off a poisonous substance and so the plant must be removed from the tank before being cut or divided. *L. sessiliflora* is also grown as an aquarium plant.

Limnobium stoloniferum (5)

A South American floating plant about 4 cm (1½ in) tall, best cultivated under bright light in very soft water at 22–28°C (72–82°F). The floating leaves grow to a length of 2 cm (¾ in). Propagation is by runners.

Lobelia cardinalis, a plant which grows under bright light

Lobelia cardinalis (2)

A North American plant cultivated under bright light in water that is not too soft, at a maximum temperature of 24°C (75°F). The substrate should contain some loam. Propagation is by cuttings.

Limnophila indica, a plant with fine feathery leaves

Limnophila (Ambulia) indica (4)

An aquatic plant from tropical and subtropical Asia, Australia and Africa, with feathery leaves.

Ludwigia natans, a plant with leaves of brownish-green above, reddish-violet below

Ludwigia natans (2)

A subtropical American plant best grown under bright light at a temperature not exceeding 25°C (77°F); the water should not be too soft. The leaves are brownish-green above, reddish-violet below. Propagation is by cuttings.

Microsorium pteropus, Java fern

Microsorium pteropus (1)

An undemanding plant, also known as Java fern, which does not root firmly in the substrate but

anchors itself loosely in the gravel by its rhizome. It can also be cultivated in crevices in pieces of rock or root. It can reach a height of 30 cm (11¾in) but is usually smaller. It thrives best at a temperature of 20–28°C (68–82°F) with moderate light, but should not be grown in water that is too soft. Propagation is by daughter plantlets.

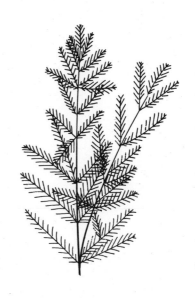

Myriophyllum brasiliense, a plant with feathery leaves

Myriophyllum brasiliense (4)

A plant with feathery leaves requiring bright light, but not too high a temperature as it comes from subtropical rather than tropical areas (maximum 25°C or 77°F). The water should not be too soft. Propagation is by cuttings. Related species, known colloquially as milfoils, also suitable for the aquarium include *M. heterophyllum*, *M. hippuroides* and *M. scabratum*.

Najas kingii, a tropical plant which can be grown in small groups

Najas kingii (4)

A brittle tropical plant from south-east Asia which requires bright light and soft water, but not at too high a temperature.

Nomaphila stricta, an attractive plant, but prone to attack by snails

Nomaphila stricta (1)

A plant from Indonesia and south-east Asia which can be cultivated under bright light at a temperature of 22–30°C (72–86°F), in water

that is not soft. It normally grows quite rapidly. Cuttings can be inserted in sand, without loam.

Nymphaea daubenyana, a water-lily

Nymphaea daubenyana (6)

One of the water-lilies, a group represented in temperate as well as tropical waters. Most are too big for the average tank and require a large amount of light, but the plant shown here is smaller, with oval floating leaves which may reach a length of 20 cm (7¾ in). It should be planted in a flowerpot containing equal parts of humus, loam and coarse sand, not mixed but put into the pot in that order, starting with the humus at the bottom. The water, which should be about 30 cm (12 in) deep, must be as soft as possible and kept at a temperature of 20–30°C (68–86°F). The plants die back in winter and should then be given a period of rest at about 12°C (54°F).

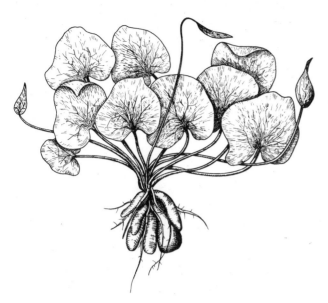

Nymphoides aquatica, underwater banana plant

Nymphoides aquatica (5)

Known as the underwater banana plant, from the shape of the roots, this plant comes from areas of shallow water in eastern North America where it lives at fairly low temperatures (not exceeding 15–22°C or 59–72°F). It can be cultivated under bright light in soft, slightly acid water, and will often live floating freely, although it is generally better to plant the tips of the roots in order to anchor it in one place.

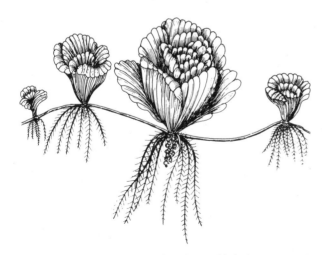

Pistia stratiotes, a very beautiful plant which does not grow too large for the average tank

Pistia stratiotes (5)

A very beautiful plant for a tank without a cover. It can be grown in shallow soft water under

bright light at a temperature of 20–30°C (68–86°F). The hanging roots provide shelter for fishes. The leaves grow to a length of 5–15 cm (2–6 in).

Riccia fluitans, a small plant which lives at the surface

Riccia fluitans (5)

A very small plant often introduced into aquaria attached to other aquatic plants. It lives at the surface and grows so rapidly that a thick cushion has to be removed every week if the submerged plants are to receive sufficient light. It thrives in soft to medium-hard water and as it needs so much light can be placed immediately below the lamps.

Sagittaria platyphylla, a suitable plant for the back of a tank

Sagittaria platyphylla (1)

Plants of the genus *Sagittaria* are widely used in the aquarium. They come from temperate and subtropical regions and so are correspondingly hardy. *S. platyphylla*, from south-eastern North America, grows to a height of 30 cm (12 in), and should be cultivated in medium-hard water, but bright light is not necessary.

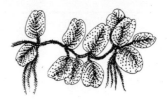

Salvinia auriculata, a rootless, floating fern

Salvinia auriculata (5)

A rootless, floating fern from tropical America, with leaves not more than 1·5 cm (approximately $\frac{1}{2}$ in) long, so this is a suitable plant for a small tank. It requires plenty of light, soft to medium-hard water at a temperature of 20–28°F (68–82°F), and does not tolerate condensation water dripping from a tank cover just above it. In fact it is best grown in an uncovered tank.

Sagittaria subulata, a plant which produces oval or spoon-shaped floating leaves

Sagittaria subulata (1)

A species from the subtropical parts of the eastern United States, which occurs in two forms. The form *natans* has leaves about 40 cm (16 in) long, whereas in the form *pusilla* the leaves only reach a length of 10 cm (3¾ in). Both forms should be cultivated under moderate light in a mixture of loam and sand, at a temperature of 25°C (77°F). The plants should then produce the oval or spoon-shaped floating leaves on long stalks.

Vallisneria spiralis, a very commonly-grown aquarium plant

Vallisneria spiralis (1)

One of the most commonly grown plants which reaches a height of 60 cm (24 in), and is sometimes confused with *Sagittaria subulata*. It should be cultivated under bright light in sand, preferably with a little loam, in medium-hard water at a temperature of 12–30°C (54–86°F). In the variety *tortifolia* the leaves are more closely twisted. There is also another larger species, *V. gigantea,* with leaves growing to a length of 1–2 m (approximately 3–6 ft).

Vesicularia dubyana, Java moss

Vesicularia dubyana (2)

Often known as Java moss, this is a widely distributed plant throughout south-east Asia, Indonesia and the Philippines. The tiny leaves, normally only 1 mm (approximately $\frac{1}{25}$ in) long, provide a good substrate for spawning. Java moss can be grown in almost any kind of water under normal tropical conditions.

4 Diets for tropical freshwater fishes

In an aquarium the plants take their nutrients from the water and the substrate. Fishes, on the other hand, cannot take nutrient in dissolved form from the water, and so they have to be fed. In general, the fishes should only be given as much food as they will consume in a few minutes. Wild fishes experience periods when food is scarce, and do not suffer if they find no food for a period of one or two days, provided, of course, that they are well fed adults, not young, growing fishes.

Provided they have been well fed in the preceding period there is no harm in leaving the fishes unfed for a couple of weeks when you go on holiday. There would need to be a time switch for the lighting so that the regular rhythm of night and day is maintained. Small algae will be growing the whole time on the plants and the glass, and when food is scarce fishes discover this nutritious vegetarian food.

Freeze-dried food contains all the necessary nutrients and is therefore very suitable for the fishes. It can be fed from an automatic dispenser and many fishes will pick the particles from the surface of the water.

In most aquarium tanks there is a hierarchy or pecking order within a species or within the community as a whole, and this is particularly noticeable at feeding time. Suddenly one fish, usually a large one, draws apart and starts to make its presence known. This 'boss' fish must feed first and the others must be made aware of

this. Young fishes should be watched under a lens in order to find out the kinds of food they prefer. Their diet can then be suitably adjusted.

Active predatory fishes require different food from peaceful species, and in larger quantities. It is useless to offer a predatory fish, known to require live food, just a few pinches of dried food. The size of the food must relate to the mouth sizes of the different fishes, although even species with a small mouth will sometimes try to swallow relatively large food.

In the aquarium world the term 'live food' is used for a wide variety of living animals which can be caught in ponds or out in the field, or bought in aquarist shops. The larger sizes of live food suitable for cichlids and large characins would include young fishes, tadpoles, hairless

Cyclops, a small crustacean seen under the microscope

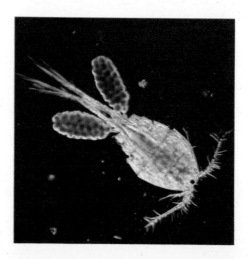

caterpillars, aquatic insects and their larvae, woodlice, earthworms, mealworms, snails, bluebottles and other large flying insects. Medium-sized live food includes mosquito larvae, *Tubifex* worms, whiteworms, small or chopped earthworms, water-fleas, small flies and maggots, and aphids. Small live food includes water-fleas and *Cyclops*, small gnat larvae, Grindal worms and microworms, and the nauplii (young stages) of the brine shrimp *Artemia salina*.

When live food is not available grated meat or chopped mussel flesh can be used. Even fishes such as the Discus, regarded as difficult to feed, will eat grated meat if it is properly prepared from beef hearts which have been carefully cleaned, leaving only the non-fatty dark red flesh. This can then be chopped up into small cubes and deep-frozen, which renders it easier to grate than raw, unfrozen flesh. The only disadvantage of this type of food is that very fine pieces fall down between the gravel to provide food for the snails.

Dried food includes the various brands sold in small containers and also oatflakes, egg yolk and dried yeast. Some species require a supplement of plant food, such as washed lettuce leaves, boiled spinach or soaked oatflakes. Very fine food for fish fry is only used in the first few days after hatching. It consists of infusorians (particularly the ciliate protozoans known as slipper animalcules or *Paramecium*), rotifers, small algae and powdered foods. The latter can be bought ready made or it can be prepared by grinding dried food. Chopped foods can be made into a kind of gruel.

Young fishes are also fond of the larvae or nauplii of *Artemia*. These small crustaceans live in waters which have a high content of mineral salts, and feed mainly on plant plankton. *Artemia* eggs are widely available on the market. When placed in water containing a level teaspoonful of cooking salt (25–30 grams) in 1 litre, or about 1 ounce in $1\frac{3}{4}$ pints of water, and kept at a temperature of 22–24°C (72–75°F) they will hatch into nauplii (singular: nauplius) in 24–36

hours. The water should be vigorously aerated to keep the eggs moving.

Freshly hatched *Artemia* should be removed from the hatching tank and kept in smaller vessels with the same type of water. They can be fed on a proprietary food such as Mikrocell, or on a suspension of yeast. The nauplii feed by filtering the tiny particles of food out of the water. Enough food should be added to make the water very slightly cloudy. As the larvae feed, the water becomes less cloudy, and when it is clear they can be given another small amount of the food. The principle here is little and often.

Fishes should be fed at the same time of day and in the same part of the tank. It will usually be sufficient to feed either in the morning or in the evening, preferably in the morning. Young fishes should normally be fed several times a day, receiving only a small portion each time.

In addition to brine shrimps (*Artemia*), other foods that can be bred include the small Grindal worms (*Enchytraeus buchholzi*) and microworms, which are even smaller, and of course whiteworms (up to $2\frac{1}{2}$ cm or 1 in long) and fruit-flies (*Drosophila*). These are not all aquatic, but some will live in the water for quite a time: microworms about 6–8 hours, Grindal worms and whiteworms up to a week in fresh water. Whiteworms should only be given as a supplementary food, perhaps twice a week. If fed too frequently the fish become fat and their readiness to spawn is impaired.

Mosquito and gnat larvae collected during the summer months from ponds or rain butts can be kept for a day or so in damp paper. If they are to be kept for longer they should be put in stoppered tubes or jars. Although these larvae are an excellent food, there is always a chance that they may complete their development and emerge as troublesome gnats or mosquitoes.

Water-fleas (*Daphnia*) should be kept in a cool place in shallow containers with the maximum surface area. The dead ones must be removed every day with a pipette and if the water is renewed every two days it is possible to keep these tiny crustaceans over a long period.

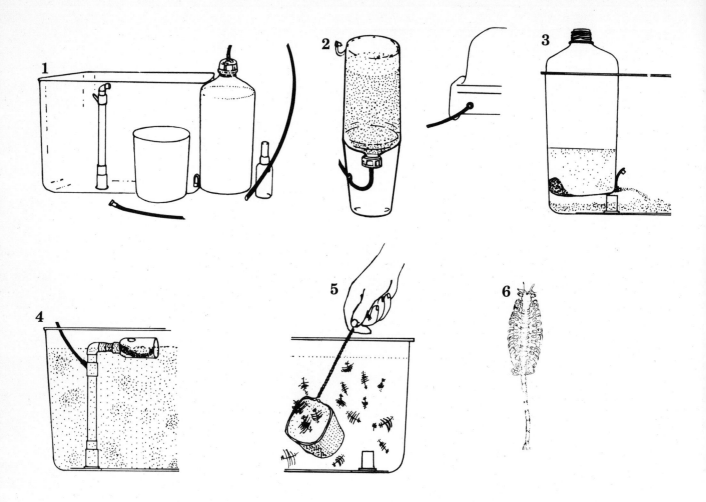

Diagram to show the hatching and rearing of brine shrimps
1) the general equipment required
2) hatching the larvae from the eggs
3) transferring larvae to the rearing tank
4) introducing food (e.g. Mikrocell) for the larvae
5) removing adult brine shrimps for feeding to the fishes
6) an adult brine shrimp

They can be fed with very small amounts of fish meal or milk and will also take any free-floating microscopic algae that are growing in the tank. When the fishes are breeding it is important to remove any water-fleas from the tank, as they may compete with the fish fry for infusorians and other microscopic foods.

Infusorians, as already mentioned, provide the smallest form of live food and are used to feed newly hatched young fishes. After hatching, most young fishes live for the first few days on the contents of their yolk sac, which forms a bulge below the body and hinders swimming. After two to three days the yolk sac contents will have been used up and the young fishes are then free-swimming. They now need a plentiful supply of very small food, which should be all around them, so that they only have to snap it up. At this time the water level in the tank can be reduced.

Infusorians should not be bred in the fish tank, but in separate small glass vessels. A culture of Paramecium can be prepared by soaking hay, or preferably turnips, in rain or pond water, leaving the vessels in good light. After two to three days large numbers of Paramecium will have been produced, giving a pink colour to the culture. Small amounts of this liquid can then be transferred into the fish tank by a spoon or pipette. Only small amounts are recommended because *Paramecium* dies quite quickly in warm water. Portions of culture should be given several times a day.

Freeze-dried food is a fairly recent introduction in the aquarium world, but is proving very useful. Almost all kinds of food can be preserved by freeze-drying, and most fishes eat it very readily. Freeze-drying involves the removal of water from the tissue.

The different types of dried food are sold in the form of flakes or powder, and are best given in a feeding ring, a small ring floating at the surface which prevents the food from spreading. The fishes soon become aware of the presence of this food and quickly consume it. It will not attract most predatory fishes, but many of the cichlids will take it quite readily. Foods that are completely unsuitable for aquarium fishes include bread, rolls, cakes, biscuits, dried ants' pupae (erroneously known as ants' eggs), and cooked potatoes. Many of these cause intestinal disturbance and they all lead to pollution of the aquarium water.

5 Fish diseases

Like all living organisms, fishes have certain defensive measures against parasites and other vectors which cause disease. Disease symptoms often appear when fish lose their resistance to such vectors. It can happen for instance if a fish suffers injury when it is being caught and taken from its natural waters. Prevention is always better than cure, although by the time damage is noticed it may have progressed too far for a cure to be possible. In general, treatment of fish diseases is a job for the experienced aquarist, but the following points should prove useful.

1. Starvation and emaciation often lead to skin lesions, which are followed by fungal infections *(Saprolegnia)*.
2. An unsuitable diet frequently causes internal troubles. This happens, for instance, when a monotonous diet low in vitamins leads to general debility or when too much fat is fed. In general, fishes do not suffer from a diet which keeps them slightly hungry.
3. Low water temperatures cause chilling and this leads to inflammation of the swimbladder and lowered resistance. Sudden changes in the temperature must always be avoided.
4. Lack of oxygen causes an increase in the respiration rate and general debility.
5. Water that is too soft or too acid does not suit all fishes. Those that live in coastal areas, such as some of the livebearers, do not tolerate very soft water or a low pH.
6. Excess sunlight, associated with a rise in the pH to 10 or more, causes cloudiness of the skin and frayed fins. The pH and hardness of the water should therefore be tested from time to time.
7. Injuries caused by apparatus or aggressive occupants in the tank become infected by bacteria or fungi.
8. Unsuitable materials used in the construction of the tank and technical equipment (e.g. metals, mastic, paint, tubing, etc.) often cause poisoning.
9. Toxic gases or vapours (e.g. from gas cookers, factory outlets, tobacco smoke, insecticides etc.) may be sucked in by the air pump and thus reach the tank water. This can be avoided by installing an air filter (with activated charcoal) between the pump and the diffuser, or by drawing in clean air from outside the room.
10. Food remains decompose rapidly and lead to an accumulation of ammonia and of nitrates.

    Steps must be taken to prevent the introduction of parasites and other disease vectors.

a. Every new fish must undergo a period of quarantine before it is put into a community tank. All sick fishes must be kept separate from the others, until completely healthy.

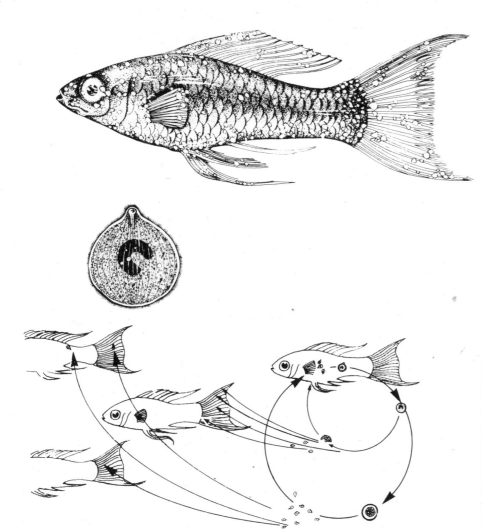

Life cycle of *Ichthyophthirius multifiliis* (white-spot). When adult, the spherical parasite on the skin of a fish falls to the bottom where it encysts. The contents of the cysts then divide to produce large numbers of motile spores which infect other fishes. At the top an infected fish is shown. Below it is a much-enlarged drawing of the adult parasite showing the typical horseshoe-shaped nucleus

b. Live food, plants and water from ponds and streams should not be used unless these are known to be clean and free from disease.

c. The substrate and all the rockwork must be thoroughly disinfected with potassium permanganate as some disease vectors have resistant spores, which can withstand heat and even desiccation.

d. Nets, glass cleaners, tubing and feeding rings must be disinfected and carefully rinsed.

e. Plants must be disinfected before being put into the tank.

f. If disease does break out, and the tank has to be emptied, the contents of the tank must be thoroughly disinfected. This includes equipment such as heaters, aerators, tubing, thermometer and filter.

6 Freshwater aquarium fishes

Family Pantodontidae (freshwater butterflyfish)

The butterflyfish *Pantodon buchholzi* is the sole member of the family, living in standing or slow-flowing waters in tropical West Africa.

Pantodon buchholzi
Butterflyfish
Length: 10 cm (3¾ in).
Characteristics: the back forms an almost straight line, indicating a surface-living fish. The mouth is deeply cleft and faces upwards.

They sometimes leave the water and glide for a short distance.
Distribution: tropical West Africa.
Aquarium conditions: a community tank at least 50 cm (20 in), containing other fishes that swim well below the surface.
Temperature: 24–30°C (75–86°F).
Diet: insects at the surface, but rarely in flight.
Sex differences: anal fin more deeply cleft in the male than in the female.
Breeding: not easy. The young are very difficult to rear.

Pantodon buchholzi, butterflyfish

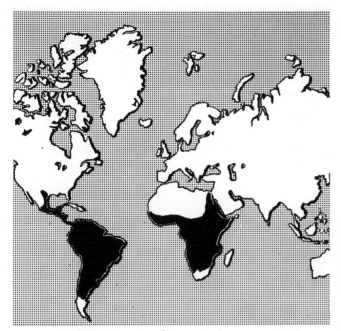

Distribution of the characin group

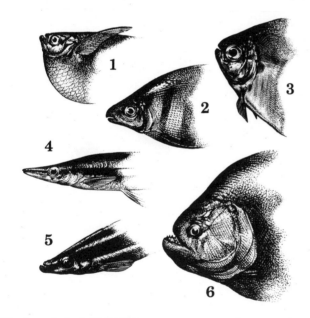

Studies of characin heads:
1) hatchetfish
2) *Distichodus*
3) *Metynnis*
4) *Phago*
5) headstander
6) piranha

Family Characidae (characins)

A widely distributed family with numerous species in Africa and in tropical America, containing many of the most popular aquarium fishes. The shape of the head and body varies considerably. Almost all the species have an adipose fin, a small fin between the dorsal and caudal fins.

Most characins are predators and so their diet in the aquarium should consist mainly of animal food. The family contains the aggressive piranhas of South America.

Pygocentrus piraya, piranha

Pygocentrus piraya
Piranha
Length: up to 60 cm (24 in).
Characteristics: an aggressive, laterally compressed fish, with long, very sharp teeth. Adipose fin present.
Distribution: South America.
Aquarium conditions: soft, slightly acid water and subdued lighting. Tank 120–150 cm (46–60 in) long.
Temperature: 24–28°C (75–82°F).
Diet: mosquito larvae and *Tubifex* for young specimens, lean meat (heart), earthworms and fish for larger individuals.
Sex differences: none externally.
Breeding: has recently been bred in captivity.
Related species are the red piranha (*Serrasalmus nattereri*), the white piranha (*Serrasalmus rhombeus*) and *Serrasalmus niger*.

47

Moenkhausia sanctaefilomenae, a characin

Gymnocorymbus ternetzi, black tetra

Moenkhausia sanctaefilomenae
Length: 6 cm (2¼ in).
Characteristics: active shoaling fishes with large scales, and an adipose fin.
Distribution: South America.
Aquarium conditions: soft, acid water (filtered through peat), and plenty of space for swimming.
Temperature: 22–26° C (71–79° F).
Diet: live food with supplementary dried food and lettuce.
Sex differences: females are larger and stouter than males.
Breeding: eggs laid at random, will be eaten if the parent fish are not removed.
The related *M. pittieri* is about the same size, but the glass tetra *(M. oligolepis)* grows to 12 cm (4¾ in).

Gymnocorymbus ternetzi
Black tetra
Length: up to 5 cm (2 in)
Characteristics: a compressed, disc-shaped fish with black areas on a greyish background. Adipose fin present.
Distribution: South America (Paraguay, Brazil, Bolivia).

Aquarium conditions: community tank from 60 cm (24 in) in length.
Temperature: 23–25°C (73–77°F).
Diet: live food with some dried food.
Sex differences: the rear end of the body cavity is pointed in the males, rounded in the females.
Breeding: is not difficult.

Pristella riddlei, X-ray fish

Pristella riddlei
X-ray fish
Length: up to 5 cm (2 in).
Characteristics: an active shoaling fish, with an adipose fin.
Distribution: northernmost South America.

Aquarium conditions: community tank from 50 cm (20 in) long, with mature water, a few plants, and subdued lighting.
Temperature: 22–26°C (70–79°F).
Diet: omnivorous.
Sex differences: male's caudal fin much redder than female's during the spawning period.
Breeding: is possible.

Aphyocharax rubropinnis
Bloodfin
Length: up to 6 cm (2¼ in).
Characteristics: a shoaling fish, with adipose fin, usually swimming near the surface.
Distribution: South America (Argentina).
Aquarium conditions: community tank from 40 cm (16 in) in length.
Temperature: 22–28°C (72–82°F).
Diet: omnivorous.
Sex differences: females are stouter than males.
Breeding: is not too difficult.

Paracheirodon innesi, neon tetra

Paracheirodon innesi
Neon tetra
Length: about 4 cm (1½ in).
Characteristics: a peaceful characin, with an adipose fin, usually swimming in the middle water layers.

Distribution: South America (upper Amazon).
Aquarium conditions: community tank at least 40 cm (16 in) in length, with clumps of dense vegetation.
Temperature: 21–25°C (70–77°F).
Diet: live food, with some dried food and lettuce.
Sex differences: females are stouter than males.
Breeding: is possible.

Cheirodon axelrodi, cardinal tetra

Cheirodon axelrodi
Cardinal tetra
Length: up to 4 cm (1½ in).
Characteristics: a peaceful and hardy characin, with an adipose fin.
Distribution: South America (upper Rio Negro).
Aquarium conditions: community tank at least 40 cm (16 in) long, with some plants.
Temperature: 23–25°C (73–77°F).
Diet: live and dried food.
Sex differences: females are stouter than males.
Breeding: is possible.

Hemigrammus erythrozonus
Glowlight tetra
Length: up to 5 cm (2 in)
Characteristics: an attractive, usually territorial characin, with an adipose fin.
Distribution: northern South America.

Aphyocharax rubropinnis, bloodfin

Hemigrammus erythrozonus, glowlight tetra

Aquarium conditions: community tank with patches of dense vegetation.
Temperature: 24–28°C (75–82°F).
Diet: live food with some dried food and lettuce.
Sex differences: females are stouter than males, and usually larger.
Breeding: not easy.

Petitella georgiae, a shoaling characin

Petitella georgiae
Length: up to 5 cm (2 in).
Characteristics: an elegant shoaling characin with an adipose fin.

Distribution: South America (upper Amazon).
Aquarium conditions: soft acid water in a community tank about 40 cm (16 in) long.
Temperature: about 24°C (75°F).
Diet: live food with some dried food and lettuce.
Sex differences: females are larger and stouter than males.
Breeding: evidently not yet bred in captivity.

Hyphessobrycon callistus, blood characin or jewel tetra

Hyphessobrycon callistus
Blood characin
Length: up to 4 cm (1½ in).
Characteristics: an active, territorial characin with an adipose fin. There are several varieties of this species.
Distribution: South America.
Aquarium conditions: preferably a species tank, from 40 cm (16 in). The water should be soft and slightly acid.
Temperature: about 24°C (75°F).
Diet: mainly live food with a small amount of dried food.
Sex differences: females stouter, males more brightly coloured.
Breeding: is possible.

Hyphessobrycon rubrostigma, bleeding heart tetra

Hyphessobrycon rubrostigma
Bleeding heart tetra
Length: 8 cm (3 in).
Characteristics: a hardy characin with a 'heart' marking and an adipose fin.
Distribution: South America.
Aquarium conditions: a community tank about 50 cm (20 in) long with soft, slightly acid water.
Temperature: about 24°C (75°F).
Diet: mainly live food, with some dried food.
Sex differences: males are more colourful, females stouter.
Breeding: is possible.

Hyphessobrycon ornatus
Length: up to 6 cm (2¼ in).
Characteristics: a hardy shoaling characin, with an adipose fin, which usually swims fairly close to the bottom.
Distribution: South America (Guyana).
Aquarium conditions: community tank from 40 cm (16 in) long, with soft, slightly acid water and clumps of dense vegetation.
Temperature: about 24°C (75°F).

Hyphessobrycon ornatus, a hardy shoaling characin

Diet: live food, with dried food and lettuce.
Sex differences: the dorsal fin is more elongated in the males. Females stouter.
Breeding: is possible.

Astyanax jordani, blind cave characin, subterranean form

Astyanax jordani
Blind cave characin
Length: up to 7 cm (2¾ in).
Characteristics: a blind, shoaling characin with an adipose fin.
Distribution: underground waters in the cave area of the Rio Panuco at San Luis Potosi, Mexico.
Aquarium conditions: a community tank from 60 cm (24 in) long with subdued lighting and some rockwork.
Temperature: about 22°C (72°F).
Diet: live food with some dried food.
Sex differences: the fins are sometimes slightly pigmented, but not in the females.
Breeding: is not difficult.

Ephippicharax orbicularis
Length: up to 12 cm (4¾ in).
Characteristics: a hardy, shoaling characin with an adipose fin.
Distribution: eastern South America (Guyana to Rio Grande do Sul and Paraguay).
Aquarium conditions: community tank from 70 cm (28 in) long with some vegetation, but leaving sufficient open water for swimming.

Ephippicharax orbicularis, a hardy shoaling characin

Temperature: about 24°C (75°F).
Diet: live and dried food.
Sex differences: none.
Breeding: is difficult but has been achieved in captivity.

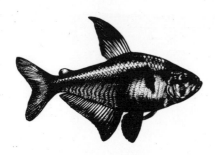

Megalamphodus sweglesi, a hardy shoaling characin

Megalamphodus sweglesi
Length: up to about 4·5 cm (1¾in).
Characteristics: a hardy shoaling characin with an adipose fin.
Distribution: South America (Amazon basin).
Aquarium conditions: community tank from 40 cm (16 in) with clumps of plants and subdued lighting.
Temperature: 24–26°C (75–79°F).
Diet: mainly live food with some dried food.
Sex differences: males with an elongated, pointed dorsal fin, females stouter.
Breeding: has been achieved.

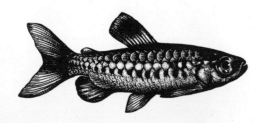

Arnoldichthys spilopterus, red-eyed characin

Arnoldichthys spilopterus
Red-eyed characin
Length: up to 7 cm (2¾in).
Characteristics: a hardy, shoaling characin, with an adipose fin and conspicuously large scales.
Distribution: West Africa.
Aquarium conditions: a community tank about 60 cm (24 in) long with soft water and some plants.
Temperature: about 25°C (77°F).
Diet: mainly live food, including earthworms, and some dried food.

Sex differences: males are more brightly coloured than females.
Breeding: evidently not yet bred in the aquarium.

Micralestes interruptus, Congo tetra

Micralestes interruptus
Congo tetra
Length: 8 cm (3in).
Characteristics: a hardy characin, with an adipose fin. Formerly known as *Phenacogrammus interruptus.*
Distribution: West Africa.
Aquarium conditions: community tank about 60 cm (24 in) long, with a few plants and soft, slightly acid water.
Temperature: 24–26°C (75–79°F).
Diet: mainly live food, with a supplement of dried food and lettuce.
Sex differences: males are larger than females and their dorsal and anal fins are more elongated.
Breeding is possible, but not easy.

Alestes longipinnis
Long-finned characin
Length: 14 cm (5½in).
Characteristics: an active, hardy, shoaling characin with an adipose fin.

Alestes longipinnis, long-finned characin

Distribution: tropical West Africa.
Aquarium conditions: community tank about 60 cm (24 in) long with soft, slightly acid water and some plants.
Temperature: about 24°C (75°F).

Diet: mainly live food, including earthworms, and some dried food and lettuce.
Sex differences: the dorsal fin is much elongated in the males.
Breeding: evidently not yet achieved in captivity.

Family Anostomidae (headstanders)

A family of South American fishes related to the characins, with a small mouth and a torpedo-shaped body. They mostly move about in an oblique position with the head down.

Anostomus anostomus, striped anostomus

Anostomus anostomus
Striped anostomus
Length: about 15 cm (5½ in).
Characteristics: an elongated fish with an adipose fin, swimming in a characteristic vertical position.
Distribution: South America (Amazon and Guyana).
Aquarium conditions: community tank at least 100 cm (40 in) long with areas of vegetation.
Temperature: 25–27°C (77–81°F).
Diet: live food and algae, with some dried food.
Sex differences: none reliable.
Breeding: evidently not yet achieved in captivity.

Chilodus punctatus, spotted headstander

Chilodus punctatus
Spotted headstander
Length: 7–8 cm (2¾ in).
Characteristics: a rather delicate species with an adipose fin.
Distribution: north-eastern South America.
Aquarium conditions: community tank at least 80 cm (32 in) long.

Temperature: 22–29°C (72–83°F).
Diet: live food, with a supplement of dried food and lettuce.
Sex differences: females are usually stouter than males.
Breeding: has been achieved.

Family Hemiodontidae
A family of small, slender South American fishes, related to the characins but with teeth only in the upper jaw. Some species have an adipose fin, others do not.

Poecilobrycon harrisoni = Nannostomus harrisoni
Length: 6 cm (2¼ in).
Characteristics: an elegant pencilfish, with an adipose fin.
Distribution: South America.
Aquarium conditions: a community tank about 40 cm (16 in) long, with areas of dense vegetation and soft, slightly acid water.
Temperature: 25–27°C (77–81°F).
Diet: mainly live food with some dried food.
Sex differences: females are slightly stouter than males.
Breeding: is difficult. Eggs are rarely produced in captivity.

Nannostomus trifasciatus
Three-banded pencilfish
Length: 6 cm (2¼ in).
Characteristics: a rather delicate pencilfish, with an adipose fin, normally swimming in the upper half of the tank.
Distribution: South America (Amazon and Guyana).
Aquarium conditions: a community tank about 40 cm (16 in) long, with soft, slightly acid water.
Temperature: 24–27°C (75–81°F).
Diet: mainly live food, but occasionally some dried food.
Sex differences: males are more brightly coloured, females somewhat stouter.
Breeding: is very difficult to achieve in captivity.

Poecilobrycon harrisoni, a pencilfish

Nannostomus trifasciatus, three-banded pencilfish

Poecilobrycon unifasciatus, one-lined pencilfish

Poecilobrycon unifasciatus (= *Nannostomus unifasciatus*)
One-lined pencilfish
Length: 6 cm (2¼ in).
Characteristics: a rather delicate pencilfish, with an adipose fin.
Distribution: South America.
Aquarium conditions: preferably a species tank about 40 cm (16 in) long, with soft, slightly acid water and areas of dense vegetation.
Temperature: 24–27°C (75–81°F).
Diet: mainly live food with some dried food.
Sex differences: the anal fin of the males has a round edge, that of the female is truncated.
Breeding: has been achieved.

Family Citharinidae
A family of tropical African fishes related to the characins. Most species are too large for the home aquarium where they are not often seen except when young. They do well on a diet of live food supplemented with some plant food.

Distichodus sexfasciatus, six-banded pencilfish

Distichodus sexfasciatus
Six-banded distichodus
Length: up to 25 cm (9¾ in).
Characteristics: a handsome shoaling fish which some may find unsuitable for the home aquarium as it has the habit of browsing on the plants. It has an adipose fin.

Distribution: tropical Africa.
Aquarium conditions: a community tank at least 60 cm (24 in) long, with decorative rocks and roots.
Temperature: 25–27°C (77–81°F).
Diet: live food, with some dried food, lettuce and algae.
Sex differences: none reliable.
Breeding: evidently not yet achieved in the aquarium.

Family Gasterosteidae (hatchet-fishes)
A small family of fishes from tropical America (Panama to southern Brazil) with a straight dorsal line and a very convex ventral line. They are able to glide over the water surface using the pectoral fins as 'wings'.

Carnegiella strigata, marbled hatchetfish, and *Carnegiella strigata vesca*

Carnegiella strigata
Marbled hatchetfish
Length: up to 4·5 cm (1¾ in).
Characteristics: a surface-living fish with a straight back and no adipose fin.

Distribution: South America (Amazon and Guyana).

Aquarium conditions: community tank from 50 cm (20 in) long with soft, slightly acid water. It must have a good lid as hatchetfishes can leave the water and glide above the surface, sometimes landing outside the tank.

Temperature: at surface 25–30°C (77–86°F).

Diet: live food with a little dried food.

Sex differences: none.

Breeding: has been achieved.

Family Cyprinidae (barbs)

A very large family with a wide distribution in North America, Europe, Asia and Africa. Coldwater species include carp, tench, chub and goldfish. Most of the tropical species kept in the home aquarium are relatively small. Most but not all barbs have one or two pairs of barbels on the lips. These have a sensory function and help the fish to find food on the bottom. With very few exceptions barbs lack an adipose fin.

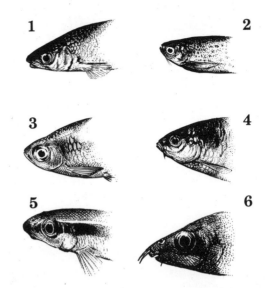

Studies of cyprinid heads:
1) *Balantiocheilus* species
2) *Brachydanio frankei*, leopard danio
3) *Rasbora heteromorpha*, harlequin fish
4) *Barbus arulius*
5) *Epalzeorhynchus* species
6) *Labeo* species

Distribution of the carp and barb family (Cyprinidae)

Carassius auratus, veiltail goldfish

Carassius auratus
Goldfish
Length: up to about 20 cm (8 in).

Characteristics: fast-growing active shoaling fish, with numerous domesticated varieties.

Distribution: China, but introduced to other parts of the world.

Aquarium conditions: community tank from 50 cm (20 in) long. A proportion of the water should be replaced at frequent intervals.
Temperature: about 15°C (59°F).
Diet: water-fleas, mosquito larvae, *Tubifex*, earthworms, algae, dried food.
Sex differences: anal area slightly concave in the male, convex in the female.
Breeding: easy.

Brachydanio frankei, leopard danio

Aquarium conditions: community tank from 30 cm (12 in) long, with good lighting, and preferably some sunlight.
Temperature: 23°C (73°F).
Diet: live and dried food.
Sex differences: female somewhat rounder.
Breeding: is not difficult.

Brachydanio albolineatus
Pearl danio
Length: 6 cm (2¼ in).
Characteristics: two pairs of barbels. Active in the upper and middle water layers. Very hardy.
Distribution: south-east Asia.
Aquarium conditions: community tank from 40 cm (16 in) long, with good lighting, a few plants and open water for swimming.
Temperature: 20–25°C (68–77°F).
Diet: live and dried food.
Sex differences: male smaller and more slender than female.
Breeding: is quite easy.

Brachydanio nigrofasciatus
Spotted danio
Length: 6 cm (2¼ in).
Characteristics: a hardy species with only one pair of barbels.
Distribution: Burma.
Aquarium conditions: community tank from 30 cm (12 in) long, with a few plants and open water.
Temperature: about 23°C (73°F).
Diet: live and dried food.

Balantiocheilus melanopterus, a tropical barb

Balantiocheilus melanopterus
Length: up to 25 cm (10 in).
Characteristics: a predatory, shoaling species. Liable to jump out of the water.
Distribution: south-east Asia.
Aquarium conditions: community tank from 70–80 cm (28–32 in) long, with a large area for swimming, and a close-fitting lid.
Temperature: 24–26°C (75–79°F).
Diet: omnivorous, e.g. water-fleas, *Tubifex*, mosquito larvae, dried food.
Sex differences: females are stouter than males.
Breeding: evidently not yet bred in the aquarium.

Brachydanio frankei
Leopard danio
Length: 6 cm (2¼ in).
Characteristics: two pairs of barbels. An active fish in the upper and middle water layers.
Distribution: south-east Asia.

Brachydanio albolineatus, pearl danio

Brachydanio nigrofasciatus, spotted danio

Sex differences: females are usually stouter.
Breeding: is not difficult.

Brachydanio rerio, zebra danio

Brachydanio rerio
Zebra danio
Length: 6 cm (2¼ in).
Characteristics: two pairs of barbels. A very hardy, active fish.
Distribution: eastern parts of the Indian subcontinent.
Aquarium conditions: community tank from 40 cm (16 in) long, with some plants, good

lighting and areas of open water for swimming.
Temperature: 18–25°C (64–77°F).
Diet: live and dried food.
Sex differences: female larger and stouter than male.
Breeding: easy.

Danio malabaricus, giant danio

Danio malabaricus
Giant danio
Length: up to 15 cm (6 in).
Characteristics: active fish which must be kept in a shoal, when they will swim mostly in the upper water layers.
Distribution: Sri Lanka and western India.
Aquarium conditions: community tank from 50 cm long, with a few tough plants and an extensive area of open water.
Temperature: 20–25°C (68–77°F).
Diet: water-fleas, mosquito larvae, *Tubifex*, fruit-flies, dried food.
Sex differences: the central blue stripe runs straight in the male, but bends up at the rear end in the female.
Breeding: is not difficult. The parents should be removed after spawning to prevent them eating the eggs, a habit that is all too common among barbs and many other aquarium fishes.

Epalzeorhynchus kalopterus
Length: up to 10 cm (3¾ in).
Characteristics: an attractively marked, slender barb with one pair of barbels.

Epalzeorhynchus kalopterus, a barb

Distribution: south-east Asia.
Aquarium conditions: community tank at least 60 cm (24 in) long, with soft water, and some plants. Decorative rocks and roots will act as sites for the growth of algae. The type of water is not critical.
Temperature: about 24°C (75°F).

Diet: live and dried food, with algae.
Sex differences: none known.
Breeding: has evidently not been recorded in captivity.

Labeo bicolor
Red-tailed labeo
Length: up to 20 cm (8 in).
Characteristics: a somewhat aggressive territorial fish.
Distribution: south-east Asia (Malaya, Thailand).
Aquarium conditions: community tank from 50 cm (20 in) long, but arranged so that each fish can take up a separate territory. The water should be soft and slightly acid.
Temperature: 24–26°C (75–79°F).
Diet: water-fleas, *Tubifex*, mosquito larvae, algae, lettuce leaves.
Sex differences: females larger than males.
Breeding: is possible.

Labeo bicolor, red-tailed labeo

Labeo frenatus, labeo

Labeo frenatus

Length: up to 8 cm (3¼ in).

Characteristics: an aggressive territorial fish. Two pairs of barbels.

Distribution: south-east Asia (Thailand).

Aquarium conditions: community tank from 50 cm (20 in) long, but a larger size is preferable. The water should have a hardness up to 10° DH.

Temperature: 24–26°C (75–79°F).

Diet: water-fleas, *Tubifex*, algae, dried food, lettuce.

Sex differences: female stouter than male. Anal fin with a black edge in the male.

Breeding: evidently not yet bred in the aquarium.

Barbus barilioides
Angola barb

Length: up to 8 cm (3¼ in).

Characteristics: an active barb swimming mostly in the lower half of the tank.

Distribution: tropical West Africa (Angola).

Aquarium conditions: community tank from 50 cm (20 in) long, with some vegetation and open water for swimming in the middle. Some shade should be supplied, possibly by floating plants.

Temperature: about 23°C (73°F).

Diet: *Tubifex*, water-fleas, mosquito larvae, dried food, lettuce.

Sex differences: females are stouter than the males.

Barbus barilioides, Angola barb

Breeding: evidently not yet bred in the aquarium.

Barbus conchonius
Rosy barb

Length: up to 14 cm (5½ in) long.

Characteristics: a hardy barb, lacking barbels.

Distribution: eastern part of the Indian subcontinent.

Aquarium conditions: community tank from 70 cm (28 in) long with a soft substrate and a few plants round the edges. Some of the water should be renewed regularly.

Barbus conchonius, rosy barb

Temperature: 18–25°C (64–77°F).
Diet: water-fleas, *Tubifex*, dried food, lettuce.
Sex differences: females stouter than males and not so brightly coloured.
Breeding: one of the easiest barbs to breed, and very prolific. The parents must be separated from the eggs immediately after spawning.

Barbus lateristriga, spanner barb

Barbus lateristriga
Spanner barb
Length: up to 20 cm (7¾ in).
Characteristics: a hardy barb, with two pairs of

barbels, which spends most of the time in the lower water layers.
Distribution: Malaya, Greater and Lesser Sunda Islands.
Aquarium conditions: community tank from 70 cm (28 in) long, with plants round the edges and a soft substrate. The water should be medium-hard.
Temperature: about 23°C (73°F).
Diet: water-fleas, *Tubifex*, mosquito larvae and some dried food as well as lettuce.
Sex differences: female stouter than male.
Breeding: is possible.

Barbus nigrofasciatus
Black ruby
Length: 6 cm (2¼ in).
Characteristics: no barbels. A hardy barb which should be kept as a small shoal, which will swim mainly in the middle water layers.
Distribution: Sri Lanka.
Aquarium conditions: community tank from 50 cm (20 in) long, with a soft substrate and some plants, but there must be sufficient open water for swimming.

Barbus nigrofasciatus, black ruby barb

Barbus oligolepis, island barb

Temperature: 22–28°C (72–82°F).
Diet: water-fleas, mosquito larvae, dried food, lettuce.
Sex differences: males more brightly coloured than females and with a black dorsal fin. Females stouter.
Breeding: is possible.

Barbus oligolepis
Island barb
Length: 5 cm (2 in).
Characteristics: one pair of barbels.
Distribution: south-east Asia (Sumatra).
Aquarium conditions: community tank from 40 cm (16 in) long, with marginal vegetation and a soft substrate.
Temperature: 23°C (73°F).
Diet: water-fleas, *Tubifex*, mosquito larvae, dried food, lettuce.
Sex differences: the male's dorsal fin has a black border.
Breeding: is possible.

Barbus tetrazona, Sumatra or tiger barb

Barbus tetrazona
Sumatra or tiger barb
Length: up to 7 cm (2¾ in).
Characteristics: a hardy barb best kept as a shoal, but liable to nibble the fins of other species.
Distribution: south-east Asia (Thailand, Sumatra, Borneo).

Aquarium conditions: community tank from 50 cm (20 in) long with a soft substrate and a few plants leaving ample space for swimming.
Temperature: 22–25°C (72–77°F).
Diet: water-fleas, *Tubifex*, dried food, lettuce.
Sex differences: male shows more red coloration. Female a little larger.
Breeding: is possible.

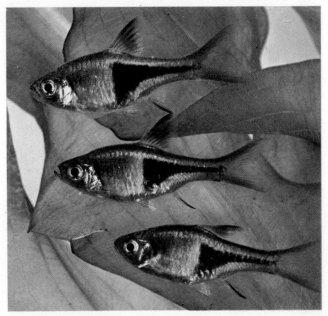

Rasbora heteromorpha, harlequin fish

Rasbora heteromorpha
Harlequin fish
Length: 4·5 cm (1¾ in).
Characteristics: a rather delicate fish with a conspicuous dark, wedge-shaped marking at the rear of each flank.
Distribution: south-east Asia (Malaya, Thailand, Sumatra).
Aquarium conditions: soft, slightly acid water in a tank with subdued lighting.
Temperature: about 24°C (75°F).
Diet: live and dried food.
Sex differences: larger and stouter female has front edge of wedge-shaped marking straight, whereas in male it is rounded.
Breeding: is possible, but the water must be soft.

Barbus titteya, cherry barb

Barbus titteya
Cherry barb
Length: 5 cm (2 in).
Characteristics: one pair of barbels.
Distribution: Sri Lanka.
Aquarium conditions: community tank from 40 cm (16 in) long with plants and open water.
Temperature: 24–26°C (75–79°F).
Diet: water-fleas, *Tubifex*, dried food, lettuce.
Sex differences: males more brightly coloured than females.
Breeding: is possible.

Rasbora trilineata
Scissors-tail
Length: up to 15 cm (6 in).
Characteristics: a hardy, shoaling fish with a scissoring action of the caudal fin lobes.
Distribution: south-east Asia (Malaya, Sumatra, Borneo).
Aquarium conditions: community tank from 60 cm (24 in) long with plenty of open water for swimming.

Rasbora trilineata, scissors-tail

Temperature: 20–25°C (68–77°F).
Diet: live and dried food.
Sex differences: females are stouter than males.
Breeding: is not difficult.

Other rasboras, all from south-east Asia, that can be kept in the same way include the Eye-spot Rasbora *(Rasbora dorsiocellata)*, up to 7 cm (2¾ in), the Spotted Rasbora *(R. maculata)*, 2·5 cm (1 in), *R. kalochroma* and *R. lateristriata*, both up to 12 cm (4¾ in), and the very small *R. urophthalma*, up to 2·5 cm (1 in).

Family Mormyridae (elephant-trunk fishes)

A small family of African fishes, many of which have the mouth elongated to form a proboscis.

Head of a mormyrid, an elephant-trunk fish

They feed mainly on small worms taken from the substrate. Mormyrids produce weak electric pulses which serve in direction-finding.

Gnathonemus petersi
Length: about 20 cm (8 in).
Characteristics: snout elongated to form a proboscis, hence the popular name of elephant-trunk fishes for the family.

Gnathonemus petersi, an elephant-trunk fish

Distribution: Africa (Niger to Zaire).
Aquarium conditions: spacious tank with numerous hiding-places. It is best not to keep several specimens in the same tank. Frequent renewals of a proportion of the water.
Temperature: 24°C (75°F).
Diet: small worms and other live food, with occasional dried food.
Sex differences: none.
Breeding: not yet achieved in the aquarium.

Family Gyrinocheilidae

A very small family of Asiatic fishes, with only three species, all in the genus *Gyrinocheilus*. They have a suctorial mouth which enables them to attach themselves to rocks and to feed on algae. There is an additional aperture above the gill opening which enables water to reach the gills when the mouth is attached to a rock.

Gyrinocheilus aymonieri
Length: up to 25 cm (9¾ in), but not so large in the aquarium.
Characteristics: bottom-living fishes with a suctorial mouth with which they attach themselves to rocks, or in the aquarium to the glass panes, which they help to keep clear of algae.

Gyrinocheilus aymonieri

Distribution: south-east Asia (Thailand).
Aquarium conditions: a community tank from 50 cm long with rocks and roots, and clear water with a high oxygen content.
Temperature: 22–28°C (72–82°F).
Diet: mainly algae, but dried food is also taken.
Sex differences: none recorded.
Breeding: not yet recorded in the aquarium.

Family Cobitidae (loaches)

A family of bottom-living fishes widely distributed in the Old World. They have an erectile spine in front of each eye and a ventrally positioned mouth with which they take algae from rocks and worms and insect larvae from the bottom. Loaches come to the surface from time to time and swallow air which passes backwards to the gut. The oxygen in the air is absorbed by the walls of the hind-gut. This respiratory method allows loaches to live in waters deficient in oxygen.

Botia hymenophysa, tiger loach

Acanthopthalmus species, kuhli, or coolie, loach

Acanthophthalmus species.
Length: up to 8 cm (3 in).
Characteristics: eel-like bottom-living fishes with an erectile spine in front of each eye. Three pairs of barbels. There are several species or subspecies, all rather similar to one another.
Distribution: south-east Asia.
Aquarium conditions: species tank about 40 cm (16 in) long with plants, subdued lighting and hiding-places.
Temperature: 24–28°C (75–82°F).
Diet: *Tubifex*, whiteworms, lettuce, dried food.
Sex differences: females are stouter than males.
Breeding: not known to have bred in captivity.

Botia hymenophysa
Tiger loach
Length: up to 25 cm (9¾ in), but not so long in the aquarium.
Characteristics: a hardy, nocturnal loach, living most of the time near the bottom. Three pairs of barbels.

Distribution: south-east Asia (Thailand, Malaya, Java, Sumatra, Borneo).
Aquarium conditions: a species tank from 40 cm (16 in) long is preferable, but can be kept in a community tank with larger fishes.
Temperature: 24–28°C (75–82°F).
Diet: *Tubifex*, water-fleas, algae.
Sex differences: none known.
Breeding: not yet recorded in the aquarium.

Botia macracantha
Clown loach
Length: up to about 25 cm (9¾ in).
Characteristics: a bottom-living loach, that is active by day as well as by night. Four pairs of barbels. Very peaceful towards one another.
Distribution: south-east Asia (Sumatra, Borneo).
Aquarium conditions: preferably a species tank from 50 cm (20 in) in length. Soft water.
Temperature: 24–28°C (75–82°F).
Diet: *Tubifex*, whiteworms, water-fleas, algae.
Sex differences: none known.
Breeding: not yet achieved in the aquarium.

Acanthopsis choirorhynchus
Length: up to 18 cm (7 in).
Characteristics: a nocturnal loach, prone to digging up the substrate and uprooting the plants.
Distribution: south-east Asia (Java, Sumatra, Borneo).

Botia macracantha, clown loach

Acanthopsis choirorhynchus, a nocturnal loach

Aquarium conditions: community tank from 50 cm (20 in) long with soft water.
Temperature: about 25°C (77°F).
Diet: whiteworms, *Tubifex*, water-fleas, dried food.
Sex differences: none known.
Breeding: not yet achieved in the aquarium.

Various catfish families

There are about 2,000 catfish species, classified in about 20 families. They have one or more pairs of barbels, which in some species are very long. Catfishes live on or near the bottom and with a few exceptions all come from fresh waters. Many are too large for the home aquarium, but there are still plenty of species which thrive in such an environment.

above: *Synodontis angelicus*, catfish
below: *Synodontis flavitaeniatus*, catfish

Synodontis angelicus
Length: up to 20 cm (7¾ in).
Characteristics: a nocturnal catfish with brilliant coloration when young, but becoming duller with age.
Distribution: tropical West Africa.
Aquarium conditions: community tank from 60 cm (24 in) long, preferably with soft water,

although they will tolerate medium-hard water.
Temperature: 23–27°C (73–81°F).
Diet: omnivorous.
Sex differences: none known:
Breeding: probably not yet achieved.
The related *S. flavitaeniatus*, also from tropical West Africa, requires the same aquarium conditions.

Synodontis nigriventris, upside-down catfish

Synodontis nigriventris
Upside-down catfish
Length: up to 6 cm (2¼ in).
Characteristics: a nocturnal catfish which swims on its back. The belly is darker than the back.
Distribution: Africa (Zaire).
Aquarium conditions: community tank from 60 cm (24 in) long, with some vegetation and plenty of space for swimming.
Temperature: 23–27°C (73–81°F).
Diet: omnivorous.
Sex differences: female stouter than male.
Breeding: probably successful in a few cases, when conditions are favourable.

Kryptopterus bicirrhis, glass catfish

Kryptopterus bicirrhis
Glass catfish
Length: up to 10 cm (3¾ in).
Characteristics: a very peaceful, transparent catfish, with one pair of long, filamentous barbels.
Distribution: south-east Asia (Thailand, Java, Sumatra, Borneo).
Aquarium conditions: community tank from 50 cm (20 in) long, provided the other fishes are not aggressive.
Temperature about 24°C (75°F).
Diet: *Tubifex*, whiteworms, water-fleas; dried food can be offered, but it may not be eaten.
Sex differences: none.
Breeding: not known to have bred in the aquarium.

Mystus vittatus
Length: up to 20 cm (7¾ in).
Characteristics: a nocturnal, bottom-living catfish with three pairs of very long barbels and an adipose fin.
Distribution: south-east Asia (India, Burma, Thailand).
Aquarium conditions: this species is really only suitable for the home aquarium when it is young. Community tank with rocks and some vegetation.
Temperature: 20–25°C (68–77°F).
Diet: earthworms, *Tubifex*, water-fleas, lettuce and some dried food.
Sex differences: none.
Breeding: evidently not yet recorded in the aquarium.

Bunocephalus kneri
Length: about 12 cm (4¾ in).
Characteristics: shaped like a frying-pan, the head and body forming the pan, the long tail the handle. Skin surface covered with numerous large tubercles. Three pairs of barbels.

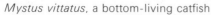
Mystus vittatus, a bottom-living catfish

Bunocephalus kneri, a catfish

Distribution: South America (Amazon basin).
Aquarium conditions: community tank about 60 cm (24 in) in length, with a soft substrate and numerous hiding-places. The fish like to burrow in the bottom.
Temperature: 20–25°C (68–77°F).
Diet: *Tubifex*, whiteworms, some dried food.
Sex differences: none known.
Breeding: not yet recorded in captivity.

Corydoras aeneus, bronze corydoras

Corydoras aeneus
Bronze corydoras
Length: up to 7 cm (2¾ in).
Characteristics: a squat, bottom-living catfish, with two pairs of barbels and an adipose fin supported by a spine.
Distribution: South America (Venezuela to La Plata) and Trinidad.
Aquarium conditions: community tank from 50 cm (20 in) in length with sand on the bottom.

Temperature: about 24°C (75°F).
Diet: *Tubifex*, water-fleas, some dried food. These fish also act as useful scavengers, picking up scraps left by others.
Sex differences: female stouter and usually larger than male.
Breeding: is possible. Two or three males can be put in a separate tank with a single female that is ready to spawn. The water temperature should be raised to 26°C (79°F). Spawning can often be induced by renewing a proportion of the water. Breeding is best attempted during the winter months.

Corydoras arcuatus, arched corydoras

Corydoras arcuatus
Arched corydoras
Length: up to 7 cm (2¾ in).
Characteristics: dorsal fin very tall and pointed.
Distribution: South America (middle Amazon).
Aquarium conditions: as for Bronze corydoras.
Temperature: about 24°C (75°F).
Diet: *Tubifex*, water-fleas, dried food and debris.
Sex differences: female stouter and usually larger.
Breeding: is possible.

Corydoras julii
Leopard corydoras
Length: up to 6 cm (2¼ in).
Characteristics: patterned with rows of fine dots, but lacking the dark band running through the eye in *C. melanistius*.

Corydoras julii, leopard corydoras

Corydoras myersi, Myers' corydoras

Distribution: South America (eastern Brazil).
Aquarium conditions: as for Bronze corydoras.
Temperature: about 24°C (75°F).
Diet: as for Bronze corydoras.
Sex differences: females stouter and usually larger than males.
Breeding: is possible.

Corydoras myersi
Myers' corydoras
Length: up to 6 cm (2¼ in).
Characteristics: a peaceful, shoaling catfish, with three pairs of barbels and an adipose fin. The dorsal dark longitudinal band extends only to the top of the head, whereas in *C. arcuatus* it extends down to the snout.
Distribution: South America (upper Amazon).
Aquarium conditions: as for Bronze corydoras.
Temperature: about 24°C (75°F).
Diet: as for Bronze corydoras.
Sex differences: female stouter and longer.
Breeding: is possible. See Bronze corydoras.

Corydoras melanistius, black-spotted corydoras

Corydoras melanistius
Black-spotted corydoras
Length: up to 7 cm (2¾ in).
Characteristics: with a pattern of fine dots, and a dark band running through the eye.
Distribution: northern South America.
Aquarium conditions: as for Bronze corydoras.
Temperature: about 24°C (75°F).
Diet: as for Bronze corydoras.
Sex differences: females are stouter and longer.
Breeding: is possible. See Bronze corydoras.

Corydoras hastatus, dwarf corydoras

Corydoras hastatus
Dwarf corydoras
Length: 3–4 cm (up to 1½ in).
Characteristics: two pairs of barbels and an adipose fin.
Distribution: South America (Amazon).

Aquarium conditions: as for Bronze corydoras.
Temperature: 24°C (75°F).
Diet: as for Bronze corydoras.
Sex differences: females are stouter and longer.
Breeding: possibly not yet bred in the aquarium. The related *C. pygmaeus* has been bred.

Loricaria filamentosa, a catfish

Loricaria filamentosa

Length: up to 20 cm (7¾ in), but smaller in the aquarium.
Characteristics: head and body protected by bony plates that overlap like roof tiles. The upper caudal fin ray is very long. Mouth ventral.
Distribution: South America (Rio Magdalena in Colombia).
Aquarium conditions: community tank from 60 cm (24 in) in length, with rocks and roots on which algae will grow.
Temperature: 22–26°C (72–77°F).
Diet: *Tubifex*, mosquito larvae, lettuce, some dried food. These fish are excellent consumers of algae, but they do not attack the aquarium's decorative plants.
Sex differences: adult males have bristles at the sides of the head. Females are stouter than males.
Breeding: is possible. The fish first clean the rocks on the bottom. When laid the eggs are whitish but they become pale brown before hatching, which should take place in 8–10 days. The male fish releases the fry from the egg cases

by striking them with his fins. They should then be transferred to a separate tank with no substrate, and as soon as the contents of the yolk sac have been consumed they must be given very fine food.

Family Gobiidae (gobies)

A large family of mainly marine fishes with a few species in fresh and brackish waters. The ventral fins are fused to form a sucker.

Brachygobius xanthozona
Bumblebee fish

Length: up to 5 cm (2 in).
Characteristics: two dorsal fins, and a very characteristic pattern of black and yellow bands. There are several very closely related species in south-east Asia.
Distribution: south-east Asia (Java, Sumatra, Borneo).
Aquarium conditions: species tank from 40 cm (16 in) in length, with sufficient hiding-places. The water should be hard, with some sea water or sea salt added.
Temperature: 24–28°C (75–82°F).
Diet: *Tubifex*, water-fleas and other live food. Dried food is usually not appreciated.
Sex differences: females are larger than males.
Breeding: is possible.

Brachygobius xanthozona, bumblebee fish

Macrognathus aculeatus, a spiny eel

Mastacembelus armatus, a giant spiny eel

Family Mastacembelidae (spiny eels)

A small family of nocturnal fishes from Africa and south-east Asia, many of which live in coastal waters with a small content of salt.

Macrognathus aculeatus
Length: up to 35 cm (13¾ in).
Characteristics: a spiny eel with a row of eye-spots on each side at the rear. Lies buried in the substrate.
Distribution: south-east Asia (India, Burma, Thailand, Malaya, Java, Sumatra, Borneo).
Aquarium conditions: for small specimens a community tank from 70 cm (28 in) long with a soft bottom and some rocks to provide hiding-places. This species should only be kept with larger fishes.
Temperature: 24–28°C (75–82°F).
Diet: *Tubifex*, earthworms, fishes.
Sex differences: none, except that the females may be stouter than the males.
Breeding: evidently not yet achieved in captivity.

Mastacembelus armatus
Length: up to 80 cm (31 in), but less in the aquarium.
Characteristics: a spiny eel that is really too large for the home aquarium, where it would be an expensive consumer of other fishes.
Distribution: south-east Asia (India, Thailand to southern China and Sumatra).
Aquarium conditions: only to be kept with larger fishes.
Temperature: 24–28°C (75–82°F).
Diet: *Tubifex,* water-fleas when young, earthworms and fishes as it grows.
Sex differences: females are stouter than males.
Breeding: evidently not yet bred in the aquarium.

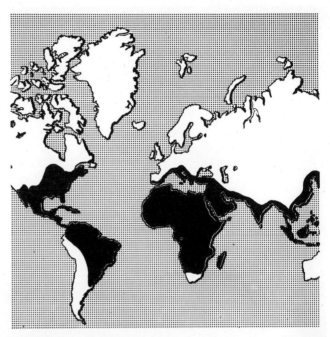
Distribution of toothcarps

Family Cyprinodontidae (egg-laying toothcarps)

A family of mainly tropical fishes with representatives in America, Africa, Asia and southern Europe. There are about 500 species, most of which are quite small. Some lay their eggs on plants, others spawn in or on the substrate. Certain species are seasonal. In these the adults die after spawning when the waters dry up. The eggs hatch in the following rainy season and the young fish mature rapidly, breed and then die within a single season.

Aplocheilus lineatus
Length: about 10 cm (3¾ in).
Characteristics: a hardy toothcarp living mainly in the upper and middle water layers.
Distribution: India and Sri Lanka.
Aquarium conditions: a tank at least 40 cm (16 in) long, with a maximum surface area and plants that grow up to produce floating leaves at the surface. These fish tend to jump so the lid must be close-fitting. Not to be kept with smaller fishes.
Temperature: 20–25°C (68–77°F).
Diet: water-fleas, *Tubifex,* flies, earthworms, fishes and some dried food.

Reproductive behaviour in toothcarps:
left: spawning on the substrate *(Epiplatys)*

centre: spawning in the substrate *(Pterolebias)*
right: mating in livebearers

Aplocheilus lineatus, an egg-laying toothcarp
above: male
below: female

Sex differences: females are smaller than males, and not so brightly coloured.

Breeding: is possible, especially if the water is filtered through peat.

Aplocheilus panchax
Blue panchax
Length: up to 8 cm (3 in).
Characteristics: a surface-living toothcarp.
Distribution: Bangladesh, Burma, Thailand, Malaya and the Greater Sunda Islands.
Aquarium conditions: a tank with a minimum length of 40 cm (16 in) and some plants. Not to be kept with smaller fishes.
Temperature: 20–25°C (68–77°F).
Diet: worms, flies, fishes and dried food.
Sex differences: the females are usually paler than the males.
Breeding: not difficult. Filtration of the water through peat is recommended.

Related species to be kept in the same way include the Green Panchax *(A. blockii),* up to 5 cm (2 in) in length, and the Ceylon Killifish *(A. dayi),* up to 9 cm (3½ in).

Aphyosemion australe
Lyretail
Length: up to 6 cm (2¼ in).
Characteristics: a handsome, but short-lived toothcarp.
Distribution: West Africa (Cameroun and Gabon).
Aquarium conditions: the tank should be about 40 cm (16 in) long, with some plants. This species can be kept in a community tank but is probably better in a species tank.
Temperature: about 22°C (72°F).
Diet: *Tubifex,* whiteworms, earthworms and some dried food.
Sex differences: males with bright coloration,

Aplocheilus panchax, blue panchax

Aphyosemion australe australe, lyretail
above and below: males
centre: female

elongated dorsal and anal fins and a lyre-shaped tail. Females smaller and duller with a rounded tail.

Breeding: is possible. This is an annual fish which hatches at the start of the rainy season, grows to sexual maturity very rapidly, pairs up and produces the next batch of eggs. The adult fish die when the waters dry up, but the eggs survive in the substrate to hatch at the next rainy season.

Aphyosemion sjoestedti
Length: up to 12 cm (4¾ in).
Characteristics: an aggressive toothcarp which attacks other fishes.
Distribution: tropical Africa (Niger delta and Cameroun).
Aquarium conditions: preferably in a species tank, about 40 cm (16 in) long, with soft, acid water.
Temperature: about 22°C (72°F).
Diet: *Tubifex*, whiteworms, earthworms, water-fleas, dried food.
Sex differences: males are more brightly coloured than females.
Breeding: is possible. The eggs hatch in approximately 100 days.

Aphyosemion sjoestedti, an egg-laying toothcarp

Epiplatys annulatus
Rocket panchax
Length: up to 4 cm (1½ in).
Characteristics: a small toothcarp living mainly near the water surface, often among floating plants. The mouth faces upwards.
Distribution: tropical West Africa (Guinea, Sierra Leone, Liberia).
Aquarium conditions: a community tank with fishes that live in the lower water layers. The water should be soft and slightly acid.
Temperature: about 24°C (75°F).
Diet: live food, including small flies, and some dried food.
Sex differences: the male's fins become red during courtship, the female remains paler.
Breeding: is possible, if the aquarist is experien-

Epiplatys annulatus, rocket panchax

ced. The male courts the female very actively, displaying his brilliant colouration and sometimes pressing her on to the spawning site. The eggs, which are attached to plants, hatch in 10–28 days.

The Firemouth epiplatys (*E. dageti,* formerly known as *E. chaperi*) can be kept in a community tank, but not with smaller fishes. It comes from Sierra Leone and Ghana and grows to a length of 6 cm (2¼ in).

Nothobranchius rachovii
Rachow's nothobranchius
Length: up to 5 cm (2 in).
Characteristics: a short-lived, rather delicate egg-laying toothcarp.
Distribution: Africa (Mozambique).
Aquarium conditions: best kept in a small species tank about 50 cm (20 in) long with shallow, very soft, acid water.
Temperature: about 24°C (75°F).
Diet: *Tubifex,* water-fleas, small fishes, insect larvae and possibly some dried food, but the latter may not be taken.
Sex differences: the females are pale brown and smaller than the males.
Breeding: is possible. The tank should have a substrate of peat fragments and contain no plants. These are seasonal or annual fishes which die at the end of the rainy season after they have spawned on the bottom. The eggs survive and produce the next brood when the rains return.
Related species, all from the coastal areas of East Africa, include *N. orthonotus* and *N. palmqvisti,* which are rather more aggressive than *N. rachovii.*

Cyprinodon macularius
Desert pupfish
Length: up to 4·5 cm (1¾ in).
Characteristics: a small egg-laying toothcarp species, in which the males show brilliant steel-like coloration.
Distribution: south-western United States.
Aquarium conditions: the tank can be quite

Nothobranchius rachovii, Rachow's nothobrachius

Cyprinodon macularius, desert pupfish

small, indeed some aquarists recommend a length of only 20 cm (7¾ in) for 4–8 specimens. There should be two to three times as many females as males. Some dense vegetation will provide shelter.

Temperature: 25–27°C (77–81°F).

Diet: water-fleas, *Tubifex* and other small live food.

Sex differences: the females are duller than the males.

Breeding: is possible.

Family Poeciliidae
(Livebearing toothcarps)

A family of small fishes from southern North America, Central and South America, most of which live in small lakes, but some in brackish estuarine waters. The anal fin of the male forms a copulatory organ, the gonopodium, with which sperm are introduced into the female's genital opening. The eggs fertilized in this way develop within the female's body and the young are born live. The sperm introduced into the female at a single mating remain viable for at least a year and serve to fertilize successive batches of eggs.

Poecilia velifera, sailfin molly, an albino form with lyretail

Poecilia velifera
Sailfin molly

Length: up to 12 cm (4¾in), but less in the aquarium.
Characteristics: active, hardy, shoaling fishes, which are fairly peaceful, but the males may be aggressive towards one another.
Distribution: central America.
Aquarium conditions: a community tank from 50 cm (20 in) long is usually quite suitable. The addition of a little sea salt is recommended.
Temperature: about 26°C (79°F).
Diet: water-fleas, *Tubifex*, mosquito larvae and other live food, with some dried food, lettuce and algae.

Sex differences: the male has a tall, sail-like fin with 18–19 rays, and a gonopodium.
Breeding: is not difficult. The females produce live young.

The closely related *P. latipinna* and the Pointed-mouth Molly, *P. sphenops*, can be kept in the same way. The mollies were formerly classified in the genus *Mollienesia*, hence the popular name.

Xiphophorus maculatus, platy

Xiphophorus maculatus
Platy

Length: up to 10 cm (3¾in), but less in the aquarium.
Characteristics: an active livebearer with a very variable pattern.
Distribution: eastern Central America.
Aquarium conditions: very easy to keep in a community tank from 40 cm (16 in) in length or even less, with clumps of dense vegetation and plenty of open water for swimming.
Temperature: 20–25°C (68–77°F).
Diet: mosquito larvae, water-fleas and other small live food, as well as some dried and plant food.
Sex differences: females have a dark pregnancy mark on the abdomen. Males have a gonopodium.
Breeding: not at all difficult. Frequently interbred with the Variatus platy, the gonopodia of the males being similar in structure.

84

Xiphophorus variatus
Variatus platy
Length: up to 20 cm (3¾ in), but less in the aquarium.
Characteristics: an active and hardy livebearer, with a varied pattern.
Distribution: Mexico.
Aquarium conditions: a community tank about 40 cm (16 in) in length with plants and open water. This and the platy are among the easiest of all tropical fishes to keep in an aquarium.
Temperature: 20–25°C (68–77°F).
Diet: water-fleas, *Tubifex* and other live food, with some dried food, lettuce and algae.
Sex differences: female with a dark pregnancy mark on the abdomen, male with a gonopodium.
Breeding: not difficult. This species interbreeds readily with the platy, and numerous hybrids are seen in the aquarium world.

Xiphophorus helleri
Swordtail
Length: up to 12 cm (4¾ in), but usually less in the aquarium.
Characteristics: active, hardy livebearers, and among the most popular of all aquarium fishes.
Distribution: Central America (Guatemala, Nicaragua).
Aquarium conditions: easy to keep in a community tank with a minimum length of 60 cm (24 in), with clumps of dense vegetation.

Temperature: 22–25°C (72–77°F).
Diet: water-fleas, *Tubifex* and other live foods, with algae, lettuce and some dried food.
Sex differences: female with a dark pregnancy mark on the abdomen. Male with a gonopodium and a characteristic long, sword-like tail.
Breeding: is not difficult. The size of the brood depends upon the size of the female. In some cases a large female will produce 150 or more live young at a time. If breeding occurs in a community tank there should be sufficient plants to provide shelter for the young. As in other livebearers a mated female can store sufficient sperm to produce several broods. Swordtails hybridize readily with other members of the genus *Xiphophorus*.

Poecilia reticulata
Guppy
Length: females up to 6 cm (2¼ in), males up to 3 cm (1¼ in).
Characteristics: active, hardy livebearers with a great number of varieties. Females are usually a uniform grey with scattered blue or green iridescence on the scales. In domesticated varieties the males show an enormous range of form and coloration.
Distribution: Trinidad, Barbados and South America north of the Amazon.
Aquarium conditions: this species is very easy to keep in a community tank, which can be quite

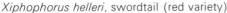
Xiphophorus helleri, swordtail (red variety)

Poecilia reticulata, two varieties with fantastic patterns

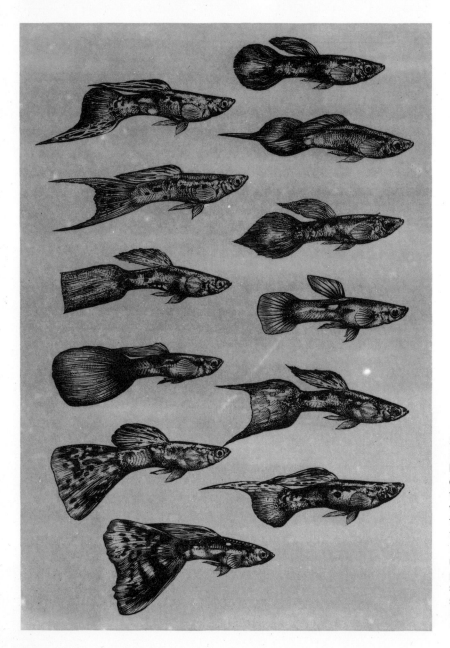

Standard forms of guppy:
Left side, from above:
bottom sword
double sword
flagtail
veiltail
fantail
triangle
Right side, from above:
round tail
pintail
speartail
spadetail
lyretail
top sword

small—from 30 cm (12 in) long. The water should not be too soft.

Temperature: about 23°C (73°F), but a few degrees lower will be tolerated.

Diet: all kinds of live food, lettuce, algae, boiled spinach, finely sieved oatmeal, as well as deep-frozen and dried food.

Sex differences: apart from their size, females are stouter and less colourful than males, which have a gonopodium.

Breeding: is very easy, the female producing broods at frequent intervals. The young should have some kind of shelter if they are born in a tank with other fishes.

Dermogenys pusillus, the common half-beak

Family Hemirhamphidae (halfbeaks)

A very small family of tropical and subtropical fishes, most of which live in sea and brackish water. Some of the halfbeaks are livebearers.

Dermogenys pusillus
Common halfbeak

Length: up to 7 cm (2¾ in), the females a little longer.

Characteristics: a sometimes rather aggressive fish, adapted for feeding at the surface.

Distribution: Burma, Thailand, Malaya, Indonesia.

Aquarium conditions: the tank should be at least 50 cm (20 in) long, so as to give as large a surface area as possible; its height is less

Lepomis gibbosus, pumpkinseed fish

important. Floating plants will provide cover as these fish tend to be nervous when first introduced to the tank.

Temperature: 26–30°C (79–86°F) at the surface.

Diet: all live foods, including flies. Some dried food will be taken, but the fish do not swim down to retrieve food that has dropped to the bottom.

Sex differences: females are larger than the males, which have the anal fin modified as a gonopodium.

Breeding: is possible, the females producing live young. Pregnant females should be moved to a separate tank with shallow water (15 cm, 6 in), and the temperature should not fall below 28°C (82°F). The brood of usually 15–40 young can be fed on the nauplius larvae of the brine shrimp *Artemia*.

The related *D. siamensis* can be kept in the same way.

Family Centrarchidae (sunfishes)

A small family of cold-water fishes from eastern and central North America. They somewhat resemble small perches. They can be kept outside in ponds provided the water does not freeze in winter.

Lepomis gibbosus
Pumpkinseed

Length: in the aquarium about 14 cm (5½ in).

Characteristics: an undemanding, temperate freshwater fish.

Distribution: North America (Great Lakes to Texas and Florida). Introduced into Europe.

Aquarium conditions: best kept in a separate species tank with a substrate of sand or gravel and groups of dense vegetation.

Temperature: 10–22°C (50–72°F).

Diet: omnivorous.

Sex differences: females normally have a greater girth and the red 'ear' patch is somewhat paler than in the male.

Breeding: is possible. The male guards the eggs until they hatch.

Family Scatophagidae (argusfishes)

A small family of laterally compressed fishes from the brackish waters of south-east Asia and northern Australia, where they live in shoals. There are two dorsal fins.

Scatophagus argus
Argusfish
Length: up to 30 cm (12 in), but usually less in the aquarium.
Characteristics: a laterally compressed, squarish fish, with two dorsal fins.
Distribution: tropical waters of the Indo-West Pacific.

Scatophagus 'rubrifrons', argus or scat fish

Aquarium conditions: community tank from 100 cm (40 in) long with decorative rocks, but no plants. A little salt should be added to the water. Filtration is recommended as large amounts of faeces are produced.
Temperature: 20–28°C (68–82°F).

Diet: probably originally vegetarian, but omnivorous in the aquarium.
Sex differences: apparently none.
Breeding: evidently not yet bred in the aquarium.
Scatophagus 'rubrifrons' is probably to be regarded merely as a variety of *S. argus*.

Family Nandidae (nandids)
A small family of predatory tropical fishes with representatives in South America, Africa and south-east Asia. They have a large protrusible mouth.

Badis badis
The badis
Length: up to 8 cm (3 in).
Characteristics: a peaceful, attractively coloured nandid, and not so voracious as other members of the family.
Distribution: India.
Aquarium conditions: the tank should be at least 40 cm (16 in) long, with decorative rockwork, clumps of dense vegetation and medium-hard water.
Temperature: 26–28°C (79–82°F).
Diet: all kinds of live food, and some dried food.
Sex differences: males have a concave belly profile, females are more convex.
Breeding: not difficult. The male protects the eggs until they hatch.

Badis badis, badis

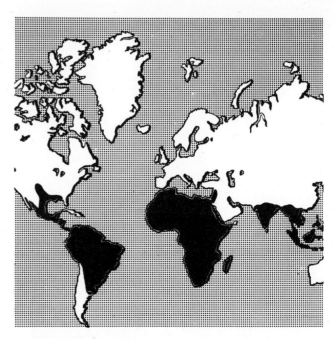

Polycentrus schomburgki, Schomburgki's leaf-fish

Distribution of cichlids

Polycentrus schomburgki
Schomburgk's leaf-fish
Length: up to 10 cm (3¾ in).
Characteristics: a voracious predatory nandid with a laterally compressed body and a protrusible mouth.
Distribution: Trinidad, Guyana, Venezuela.
Aquarium conditions: preferably a species tank from 50 cm (20 in) in length with soft, slightly acid water and groups of dense vegetation.
Temperature: 22–25°C (72–77°F).
Diet: mosquito larvae, earthworms, fishes, but after a time they may take pieces of chopped liver and heart.
Sex differences: at spawning time the males are velvety-black with blue markings, the females much duller.
Breeding: is possible. The male protects the eggs.
The related South American Leaf-fish (*Monocirrhus polyacanthus*), up to 8 cm (3 in) in length, can be kept in the same way.

Family Cichlidae (cichlids)
A large family of perch-like fishes from tropical America, Africa and southern Asia. Unlike the fishes in related families the cichlids have only a single nostril on each side of the head. They come from a wide range of aquatic habitats, some even living in brackish waters. Many of the species practise brood protection.

Apistogramma ramirezi
Ramirez's dwarf cichlid
Length: about 6 cm (2¼ in).
Characteristics: a peaceful, somewhat delicate small cichlid.
Distribution: South America (Venezuela).
Aquarium conditions: community tank about 60 cm (24 in) long, with soft, acid water filtered through peat. It should have dense marginal vegetation and rocks and roots to provide shelter.
Temperature: about 24°C (75°F).
Diet: omnivorous, but with a preference for live food.
Sex differences: males larger, more brightly coloured and with more elongated fins than the females.
Breeding: is possible. The eggs are laid in a small cavity which has been carefully cleaned. In this species both parents take part in looking after the brood. The eggs hatch in 3–4 days. The free-swimming young can be fed on *Artemia*

 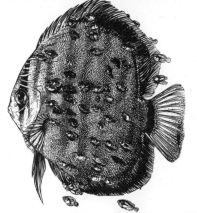 

Brood protection in cichlids:
left: substrate spawner *(Cichlasoma meeki,* firemouth cichlid), with young

centre: young discus fishes feeding on the parent's flank
right mouthbrooder *(Tilapia)* with young retreating into the parent's mouth

Apistogramma ramirezi, Ramirez's dwarf cichlid

nauplii, finely chopped *Tubifex* or whiteworms. Other dwarf cichlids with similar requirements include *Apistogramma agassizi, A. reitzigi, A. cacatuoides* and *A. wickleri.*

Astronotus ocellatus
Oscar or velvet cichlid
Length: up to 35 cm (13½in).
Characteristics: a large, robust and voracious cichlid with a handsome velvety pattern.

Distribution: South America (Amazon, Parana, Rio Negro, Rio Paraguay).
Aquarium conditions: young specimens can be kept in a community tank, but larger ones should be put into a species tank, preferably at least 100 cm (40 in) long, with soft to medium-hard water.
Temperature: 26°C (79°F), rising to 28°C (82°F) for breeding.

Astronotus ocellatus, oscar or velvet cichlid, normal form

Astronotus ocellatus, selected form known as the red oscar

broods are often large, up to 1000, but the numbers are soon reduced by cannibalism.

A coppery-red form, the Red Oscar, has recently been bred and it requires the same conditions.

Cichlasoma meeki
Firemouth

Length: up to 15 cm (6 in), but sexually mature at 10 cm (3¾ in).

Characteristics: a hardy, territorial cichlid with very brilliant coloration at spawning time, when the gill covers are spread and the bottom of the mouth and throat become a brilliant red.

Distribution: Central America (Guatemala, Yucatan).

Aquarium conditions: a community tank about 70 cm (28 in) long is usually suitable. The fish will dig up the substrate which can be medium-fine sand mixed with gravel. If plants are used for decoration they must be very firmly anchored.

Temperature: 22–24°C (72–75°F).

Diet: all kinds of live food, including earthworms, with dried, freeze-dried and deep-frozen foods as a supplement.

Sex differences: males are normally larger and more brightly coloured than females.

Breeding: is possible in a separate tank. Both

Diet: water-fleas, *Tubifex,* chopped heart, earthworms and some dried food.

Sex differences: none are really reliable.

Breeding: is not easy. Courtship is very active as the male chases the female. Both sexes should then start to clean a rock which will act as a spawning site. After hatching both parents take the young to a previously prepared pit where they remain until they are free-swimming. The

Cichlasoma meeki, firemouth cichlid

sexes clean a spawning area on the bottom. The female lays 300–400 eggs which are guarded and fanned by both parents. They hatch in about two days and the young are taken to a pit where they remain until they are free-swimming, about eight days after hatching. They should then be given plenty of food, such as *Artemïa* larvae and finely powdered dried food. The parents continue to look after them for about four weeks.

Cichlasoma octofasciatum
Jack Dempsey
Length: up to 20 cm (7¾ in).
Characteristics: an aggressive cichlid, colloquially named after the famous boxer. Young specimens are grey with only a few small blue spots. Also known as *C. biocellatum*.
Distribution: South America (middle Amazon and Rio Negro).
Aquarium conditions: this boisterous species is best kept in a species tank about 100 cm (40 in) long, with firmly fixed rockwork and floating plants.
Temperature: 20–22°C (68–72°F), rising to 26°C (79°F) for breeding.
Diet: all kinds of live food, including earthworms and small fishes, with chopped heart and dried food.
Sex differences: the forehead of the males starts to bulge as they grow older. Females are less brightly coloured.
Breeding: is not difficult. The females lay 600–800 eggs at each spawning.

Cichlasoma cyanoguttatum
Rio Grande perch
Length: up to 30 cm (12 in), but less in the aquarium.
Characteristics: a rather aggressive cichlid, with attractive coloration. Sometimes known as the Texas cichlid.
Distribution: northern Mexico and Texas.
Aquarium conditions: best kept in a species tank at least 100 cm (40 in) long without rooted plants which would not survive the fish's

Cichlasoma cyanoguttatum, Rio Grande perch

digging activities. Floating plants can be used and the area can be divided up by rocks and roots, which must be firmly fixed.
Temperature: 18–24°C (64–75°F).
Diet: live food (water-fleas, *Tubifex,* earthworms) with a supplement of lettuce.
Sex differences: only apparent as the fish age, when the males start to develop a prominent bump on the head.
Breeding: is not usually difficult. Spawning takes place on a large flat stone and the brood may contain several hundred young, which are tended by the parents.

Cichlasoma nigrofasciatum
Zebra or convict cichlid
Length: up to 10 cm (3¾ in), but sexually mature at 8 cm (3 in).
Characteristics: a relatively small but aggressive cichlid.
Distribution: Central America (Guatemala, Panama).
Aquarium conditions: a community tank 100 cm (40 in) long is suitable when the fish are

Cichlasoma octofasciatum, Jack Dempsey cichlid

Cichlasoma nigrofasciatum, zebra or convict cichlid

small, but a species tank of the same size would be better for adults. Floating plants can be used. The rockwork must be firmly fixed as these fish dig.

Temperature: 22–24°C (72–75°F).

Diet: all kinds of live food, including earthworms and snails, with lettuce and some dried food.

Sex differences: the dorsal and anal fins of the males are more elongated than those of the females.

Breeding: is possible. The water temperature should be raised a few degrees. The parent fish guard and tend the brood.

Cichlasoma salvini
Salvin's cichlid

Length: up to 15 cm (6 in).

Characteristics: a very brightly coloured cichlid, particularly during courtship and when tending the young.

Distribution: southern Mexico, Guatemala, Honduras.

Aquarium conditions: as for the Zebra cichlid.

Temperature: about 22°C (72°F), but slightly higher for breeding.

Diet: live food and some dried food.

Sex differences: the dorsal and anal fins of the males are elongated and more pointed than in the females.

Breeding: not too difficult. As for Zebra cichlid. The related Banded cichlid (*Cichlasoma severum*), up to 20 cm (7¾ in), from Guyana and the Amazon basin, is also a good aquarium fish with similar requirements.

Nannacara anomala
Golden-eyed dwarf cichlid

Length: up to 8 cm (3¼ in).

Characteristics: a small and generally peaceful cichlid that is not difficult to keep.

Distribution: South America (western Guyana).

Aquarium conditions: a community tank about 60 cm (24 in) long is suitable. It can be decorated with rocks and plants.

Temperature: 24–26°C (75–79°F).

Diet: all kinds of live food, with some dried food.

Sex differences: the females are slightly smaller than the males.

Breeding: is possible. A single male will sometimes mate with more than one female. He cleans a spawning site on the bottom. After mating the female lays her eggs on this area and carefully guards them. At this point it is

Nannacara anomala, golden-eyed dwarf cichlid

Cichlasoma salvini, Salvin's cichlid, showing breed
coloration

advisable to remove the male. After hatching the fry gather in a pit on the bottom and become free-swimming a few days later, but are still tended by the female. They can then be fed on *Artemia* nauplii and powdered food. They have a good appetite and develop rapidly.

Geophagus jurupari

Geophagus jurupari
Length: up to 25 cm (9¾ in).
Characteristics: a hardy mouthbrooding cichlid which, like others in the genus, has the habit of chewing but not swallowing the substrate.
Distribution: South America (northern Brazil, Guyana).
Aquarium conditions: species tank about 70 cm (28 in) long with a soft sandy substrate, and some rocks and roots.
Temperature: 22–28°C (72–82°F).
Diet: all kinds of live food, including earthworms.
Sex differences: females are stouter than males.
Breeding: is possible. The female takes the spawned eggs into her mouth where they remain until they hatch.

Pterophyllum scalare
Angelfish
Length: up to 15 cm (6 in).
Characteristics: a laterally compressed, very tall cichlid.
Distribution: South America (Amazon).
Aquarium conditions: a tall species tank from 70 cm (28 in) long with rockwork, a tangle of roots and a number of plants. The water should preferably be soft.
Temperature: about 24°C (75°F).
Diet: live food, lettuce and some dried food. They also eat small fishes.
Sex differences: difficult to define.
Breeding: is possible. The parent fish guard the eggs and tend the young.
The related species *P. altum* and *P. dumerilii* require the same conditions.

Pterophyllum altum, a deep angelfish

Pterophyllum scalare,
angelfishes

Symphysodon aequifasciata aequifasciata, green discus

Symphysodon aequifasciata aequifasciata
Green discus
Length: up to 18 cm (7 in).
Characteristics: a laterally compressed cichlid with beautiful markings.
Distribution: South America (upper Amazon, Tefe to Colombian border).
Aquarium conditions: species tank at least 100 cm (40 in) long, preferably larger. With a minimum of plants if the fish are to be bred. The water must be soft and acid.
Temperature: 24–30°C (75–86°F).
Diet: all kinds of live food and some lettuce. Some aquarists feed entirely on dried or freeze-dried food.
Sex differences: none reliable.

98

The species of *Symphysodon* (discus fishes) are the only aquarium fishes which feed their young on a mucus secreted by their own flanks

Symphysodon aequifasciata axelrodi, brown discus

A selected form of the turquoise discus

Symphysodon aequifasciata haraldi, blue discus

Breeding: is possible. Spawning takes place on a hard substrate. After hatching the fry remain close to the bottom until they have consumed the yolk sac contents. They then move to the flanks of the parents where they start to feed on a skin section. Later they start to take small live food.

The Brown discus, *S. a. axelrodi,* (lower Amazon, Belem to Manacapuru) and the Blue discus *S. a. haraldi* (Amazon near Manacapuru)

Symphysodon discus, the discus

are related subspecies requiring the same conditions, as does *S. discus* known as the Discus which comes from the Rio Negro area. Selected forms of *S. aequifasciata* include the Turquoise discus.

Uaru amphiacanthoides
Triangle cichlid
Length: up to 30 cm (12 in).
Characteristics: a peaceful, shoaling cichlid with an oval outline and a conspicuous dark marking on each flank.
Distribution: South America (Amazon basin and Guyana).
Aquarium conditions: species tank from 100 cm (40 in) long with soft, acid water.

Uaru amphiacanthoides, triangle or chocolate cichlid

Temperature: 26–30°C (79–86°F).
Diet: live food.
Sex differences: none are reliable.
Breeding: is possible. The young are looked after by the parents.

Haplochromis polystigma, a mouthbrooding cichlid

Haplochromis burtoni, a mouthbrooding cichlid

Haplochromis burtoni

Length: up to 12 cm (4¾in).
Characteristics: an aggressive mouthbrooding cichlid.
Distribution: tropical Africa.
Aquarium conditions: species tank at least 70 cm (28 in) long with dense planting round the edges, and a substrate of fine sand. Medium-hard water.
Temperature: 23–25°C (73–77°F).
Diet: live food, including earthworms, also chopped meat.
Sex differences: the anal fin of the male is marked with circular egg dummies (see below).
Breeding: is possible. After spawning the female takes the still unfertilized eggs into the mouth. The male swims about in front of her head. When she tries to snap at the egg dummies she naturally opens her mouth. The male immediately sheds sperm which are drawn into her mouth where they fertilize the eggs. The female guards the fry even after they have become free-swimming.

Haplochromis polystigma

Length: up to 20 cm (7¾in).
Characteristics: an aggressive mouthbrooding cichlid with a mottled and speckled pattern.
Distribution: Africa (Lake Malawi).
Aquarium conditions: species tank at least 100 cm (40 in) long with medium-hard water.
Temperature: about 24°C (75°F).
Diet: live food, including earthworms and fishes.
Sex differences: the male has more blue on the flanks.
Breeding: is possible. As for *H. burtoni*.

Haplochromis moorii

Length: up to 20 cm (7¾in).
Characteristics: a brilliant blue mouthbrooding cichlid.
Distribution: Africa (Lake Malawi).
Aquarium conditions: as for *H. burtoni*.
Temperature: about 24°C (75°F).
Diet: live food.
Sex differences: difficult to define. Both males and females develop the forehead bump.
Breeding: as for *H. burtoni*.

Aulonocara nyassae

Length: up to about 18 cm (7 in), but less in the aquarium.
Characteristics: a brilliantly coloured mouth-brooding cichlid.
Distribution: Africa (Lake Malawi).

Haplochromis moorii, a mouthbrooding cichlid

Aulonocara nyassae, a mouthbrooding cichlid

Hemichromis bimaculatus, red cichlid of jewel fish

Aquarium conditions: as for *H. burtoni*.
Temperature: about 24°C (75°F).
Diet: live food.
Sex differences: the males have brilliant blues and reds, the females are usually grey brown.
Breeding: is possible. The eggs are laid in small caves, in the aquarium often in a flowerpot, and are incubated in the female's mouth.

Hemichromis bimaculatus
Red cichlid or jewel fish
Length: up to 18 cm (7 in), but only to 12 cm (4¾ in) in the aquarium.
Characteristics: an aggressive, brilliantly coloured cichlid.
Distribution: northern tropical Africa.
Aquarium conditions: the tank should be at least 80 cm (32 in) long to provide space for the fish to set up territories. Substrate of medium-fine sand and medium gravel, with a flat stone to serve as a spawning site.
Temperature: 22–24°C (72–75°F).
Diet: plenty of live food, including earthworms, and also scraped heart and chopped fish flesh.
Sex differences: females are stouter and are more brilliantly coloured during the breeding season than the males.
Breeding: the tank should be observed during territorial fighting, and eventually it should be possible to distinguish a compatible pair. The other fish should then be removed. The pair

then clean the spawning site and after a time the female lays eggs which are immediately fertilized by the male. The fry hatch in 2 days and are then taken by the parent fish to a previously prepared pit, where they are assiduously guarded. After a further 2 days they will have consumed the yolk sac contents and can then be fed on brine shrimp nauplius larvae.

Hemichromis fasciatus
Five-spot cichlid or banded jewelfish
Length: 25–28 cm (9¾–11 in).
Characteristics: an aggressive cichlid which sets up a territory in the tank.
Distribution: tropical Africa (Senegal to Zaire).
Aquarium conditions: a species tank about 100 cm (40 in) in length, with rocks, roots and a few robust plants.
Temperature: 20–25°C (68–77°F).
Diet: all kinds of live food.
Sex differences: the ventral fins are more elongated in the males.
Breeding: is possible. The parent fish tend the young, as in *H. bimaculatus*.

Hemichromis fasciatus, five-spot cichlid or banded
jewelfish

Lamprologus brichardi, a cichlid

Lamprologus compressiceps, a cichlid, shown with dorsal fin erected

Lamprologus brichardi
Length: 10 cm (3¾ in).
Characteristics: an elegant cichlid with elongated fins.
Distribution: Africa (Lake Tanganyika).

Tropheus moorii, a mouthbrooding cichlid

Aquarium conditions: species tank at least 50 cm (20 in) long, with medium-hard, slightly alkaline water.
Temperature: 22–24°C (72–75°F).
Diet: live food, including fishes.
Sex differences: the female is smaller than the male, and not so colourful.
Breeding: this species spawns in caves, attaching the eggs to the roof. After hatching the fry remain near the cave and are guarded by both parents, particularly the male.
The related *L. compressiceps* lives among dense vegetation in Lake Tanganyika, and it requires the same aquarium conditions as *L. brichardi*. The mouthbrooding *Tropheus moorii* also comes from the alkaline waters of Lake Tanganyika.

Julidochromis ornatus
Length: about 12 cm (4½ in).
Characteristics: a yellowish territorial cichlid with dark longitudinal stripes.
Distribution: Africa (Lake Tanganyika).
Aquarium conditions: the tank should be at least 50 cm (20 in) long and have medium-hard, slightly alkaline water.
Temperature: about 24°C (75°F).

Julidochromis ornatus, a territorial cichlid

Julidochromis regani, a cichlid

Julidochromis dickfeldi, a cichlid

Julidochromis marlieri, a cichlid

Diet: mainly live food, with some dried food. The mouth is relatively small, so they must not be given large items of food.

Sex differences: the females are usually rather longer and stouter than the males.

Breeding: the females spawn in caves, and both parents tend the fry. Each brood consists of about 20–30 eggs, and these hatch in about 3 days.

Related species that can be kept in the same way include *Julidochromis marlieri, J. regani* and *J. dickfeldi.*

Pelvicachromis pulcher
Length: up to 9 cm (3½ in).
Characteristics: a peaceful cichlid, formerly known as *Pelmatochromis kribensis*.
Distribution: tropical Africa (Niger delta area).
Aquarium conditions: a community tank from 70 cm (28 in) long is usually sufficient. There should be rocks, roots and plants to provide shelter. The composition of the water is not critical, but it is advisable to add a little sea salt (2 tablespoonfuls to 10 litres or 2·2 gallons).
Temperature: about 25°C (77°F).
Diet: mainly live food, with some dried food.
Sex differences: the males have more elongated dorsal and anal fins.
Breeding: is possible. The eggs hatch in about 3 days and the fry are free-swimming quite soon afterwards. They can be fed on fine live food, starting with brine shrimp nauplius larvae.
Pelmatochromis thomasi can be kept in the same way.

Pelvicachromis pulcher, a cichlid, formerly known as
Pelmatochromis kribensis

Steatocranus casuarius, blockhead cichlid

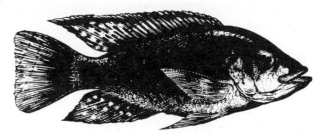

Tilapia mossambica, Mozambique mouthbrooder

Steatocranus casuarius
Blockhead cichlid
Length: 10 cm (3¾ in).
Characteristics: an aggressive, territorial cichlid, that is not too large for the home aquarium.
Distribution: Africa (Zaïre).
Aquarium conditions: in a community tank at least 60 cm (24 in) long with rocks and roots to provide hiding-places, but it is preferable to keep them in a species tank on their own.
Temperature: 24–26°C (75–79°F).
Diet: live and dried food.
Sex differences: the males develop a bulging forehead.
Breeding: is possible. Courtship and spawning are extremely vigorous. The eggs are laid in the retreat of the parent fish who both take part in guarding them. The young are still tended by the parents after they have become free-swimming and are feeding on very small live food, e.g. brine shrimp larvae.

Tilapia mossambica
Mozambique mouthbrooder
Length: 30–40 cm (11¾–15¾ in).
Characteristics: a fast-growing, rather aggressive and very hardy cichlid.
Distribution: East Africa (Nile to Natal).
Aquarium conditions: species tank at least 100 cm (40 in) long with coarse gravel and a few rocks and roots, but no plants.
Temperature: 22–24°C (72–75°F).
Diet: live and dried food, and particularly plant food.
Sex differences: the dorsal and caudal fins of the male have a red border. The male is also much darker and larger than the female.
Breeding: is not difficult. The male digs a pit at spawning time. The eggs are incubated in the mouth of the female.
This species has been introduced into south-east Asia and many other parts of the tropics as a source of human food.

Distribution of anabantids (labyrinth fishes)

Family Anabantidae
(Labyrinth fishes)
A family of tropical fishes with representatives in south-east Asia and Africa. They have an accessory respiratory organ, the labyrinth, in

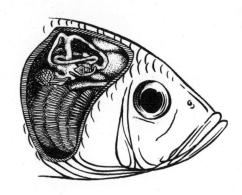

Head of an anabantid (labyrinth fish) with part of the side cut away to show the labyrinth organ above the gills

the upper part of each gill chamber, behind the eyes. The fish come to the surface and take in air which passes to the labyrinth where its oxygen is removed and used for respiration. This adaptation allows the fish to live in waters deficient in oxygen. Many species build a nest of bubbles at the surface where the male guards the eggs and fry.

Macropodus opercularis
Paradise fish
Length: 7–8 cm (2¾–3 in).
Characteristics: a brightly coloured fish with iridescent dark transverse bars.

Distribution: south-east Asia (China, Korea, Vietnam).
Aquarium conditions: can be kept in a community tank, but are better maintained in a species tank with some plants, including those that float at the surface. The water should be medium-hard.
Temperature: about 24°C (75°F).
Diet: live food, including earthworms, with algae and some dried food.
Sex differences: the fins are more elongated in the males.
Breeding: is not difficult. The male tends the brood.

Betta splendens
Fighting fish
Length: up to 6 cm (2¼ in).
Characteristics: a very colourful species in which the males are exceedingly aggressive towards one another. There are several selected varieties with veil-like fins in the males.
Distribution: south-east Asia.
Aquarium conditions: a species tank from 20–30 cm (8–12 in), or even smaller. The water should be soft to medium-hard. Plants and roots will provide shelter.
Temperature: about 26°C (79°F).

Macropodus opercularis, paradisefish

Betta splendens, fighting fish

Mating of *Betta splendens*, fighting fish, seen through the
glass bottom of an aquarium tank

Diet: live and dried food.
Sex differences: the females are smaller than the males and do not have the much developed fins.
Breeding: is not difficult. The male builds a nest of mucus-coated air bubbles at the surface and tends the brood.

Trichogaster leeri, pearl gourami

Colisa lalia, dwarf gourami

Colisa lalia
Dwarf gourami
Length: up to 5 cm (2 in).
Characteristics: a peaceful and attractively coloured anabantid that is not difficult to keep.
Distribution: Bengal and Assam.
Aquarium conditions: community tank at least 30 cm (12 in) long, with roots and some plants to provide shelter.
Temperature: about 26°C (79°F).
Diet: should be varied with live and dried food.
Sex differences: the male has elongated and pointed dorsal and anal fins.
Breeding: is possible, the male tending the brood.
Colisa chuna, up to 4·5 cm (1¾ in) long, can be kept in the same way. It comes from north-eastern India.

Trichogaster leeri
Pearl gourami
Length: about 14 cm (5½ in).
Characteristics: the ventral fins are very long and thread-like.
Distribution: south-east Asia (Thailand, Malaya, Borneo, Sumatra).
Aquarium conditions: community tank at least 50 cm (20 in) long, with sufficient vegetation and some roots to provide shelter.
Temperature: 24–30°C (75–86°F).
Diet: mainly live food, with some dried food.
Sex differences: the male has pointed dorsal fins.
Breeding: is possible, the male tending the brood.
The three-spot gourami (*Trichogaster trichopterus*) from south-east Asia can be kept under similar conditions. It also comes from south-east Asia (Thailand, Malaya, Sumatra, Java, Borneo).

Helostoma temmincki
Kissing gourami
Length: up to 30 cm (12 in).
Characteristics: an anabantid with fleshy lips occurring as two colour variants: reddish and greenish. The popular name refers to the sham fighting in which two fish appear to kiss.
Distribution: south-east Asia (Thailand, Malaya, Sumatra, Java, Borneo).

Trichogaster trichopterus, three-spot gourami

Helostoma temmincki, kissing gourami, green and pink forms

Aquarium conditions: a tank about 70 cm (28 in) long with some plants and roots to divide up the area.
Temperature: 24°C (75°F).
Diet: live and dried food, algae and lettuce.
Sex differences: none are reliable.
Breeding: is possible.

Sphaerichthys osphromenoides
Chocolate gourami
Length: up to 5 cm (2 in).
Characteristics: a delicate anabantid with filamentous pectoral fins.
Distribution: south-east Asia (Malaya, Sumatra).
Aquarium conditions: a species tank about 50 cm (20 in) long with very soft, acid water.

Temperature: 28°C (82°F).
Diet: live food.

Sphaerichthys osphromenoides, chocolate gourami

Sex differences: the dorsal fin is pointed in the male.
Breeding: is difficult. The female is said to incubate the eggs in her mouth.

Ctenopoma acutirostre
Spotted climbing perch
Length: up to 15 cm (6 in).
Characteristics: a hardy, aggressive anabantid with an oval outline.
Distribution: Africa (central Congo area).
Aquarium conditions: species tank about 70 cm (28 in) long with areas of dense vegetation.
Temperature: 24–26°C (75–79°F).
Diet: live food, including earthworms and fishes.
Sex differences: none reliable.
Breeding: evidently not yet achieved in the aquarium.

Melanotaenia maccullochi, dwarf rainbowfish

Ctenopoma acutirostre, spotted climbing perch

Gasterosteus aculeatus, three-spined stickleback

Family Atherinidae (sand smelts)

A family of mainly marine shoaling fishes, some of which live in fresh or brackish waters. They have two dorsal fins.

Melanotaenia maccullochi
Dwarf rainbowfish
Length: up to 8 cm (3¼ in).
Characteristics: a hardy, shoaling fish with two dorsal fins.
Distribution: northern Australia.
Aquarium conditions: community tank about 70 cm (28 in) long with some dense vegetation to provide shelter.
Temperature: 20–25°C (68–77°F).
Diet: live and dried food.
Sex differences: males are more colourful than females.
Breeding: is possible.

Family Gasterosteidae (sticklebacks)

A small family of cold-water fishes with representatives in North America, Europe and northern Asia. They have a varying number of sharp spines along the dorsal line. The male builds a nest and guards the eggs and young.

Gasterosteus aculeatus
Three-spined stickleback
Length: up to 10 cm (4 in).
Characteristics: a common freshwater fish with three dorsal spines.
Distribution: Europe, northern Asia, Japan, North America.
Aquarium conditions: species tank about 50 cm (20 in) long with groups of plants and good lighting.
Temperature: 16–20°C (61–68°F).
Diet: live food.
Sex differences: males are much more colourful than females.
Breeding: not difficult. The male builds a nest of plant fragments and guards both the eggs and the fry.

Family Tetraodontidae (pufferfishes)

A family of mainly marine tropical fishes with a few representatives living in fresh and brackish waters. They can inflate the body with air or water. The powerful parrot-like beak, which is formed by fusion of the teeth, makes it possible for them to crush food such as mollusc shells.

Tetraodon fluviatilis, green pufferfish

Tetraodon fluviatilis
Green pufferfish
Length: up to 5 cm (2 in) in the aquarium.
Characteristics: an aggressive fish able to inflate its body when excited.
Distribution: south-east Asia (India, Sri Lanka, Burma, Thailand, Malaya).
Aquarium conditions: species tank about 50 cm (20 in) long with plants around the edges and some rocks to provide shelter. The water must not be soft, and should contain about 3 teaspoonfuls of salt to every 10 litres (2·2 gallons).
Temperature: 22–26°C (72–79°F).
Diet: live food, with lettuce, chopped liver and grated heart. They eat snails avidly.
Sex differences: none.
Breeding: has been achieved. The male guards the brood.

7 Introduction to the tropical marine aquarium

In recent years there has been increasing interest in the maintenance of fishes and invertebrates from tropical seas. Most of these come from the coral reefs of the Indo-Pacific Ocean and the Caribbean Sea. Coral reefs are formed by the activities of countless millions of tiny coral polyps, which belong to the phylum Coelenterata (corals, sea anemones, jelly fishes). These small animals secrete calcium to form their skeletons. In addition most coral polyps contain microscopic algae, which help to colour the corals. Other algae live in between the coral stocks, and their calcareous secretions help to cement the reef. Both corals and algae require light, as well as warm, clear water rich in oxygen, hence they are found in a relatively narrow zone of tropical coastal surface waters.

In addition to the marine fishes, pieces of living coral are imported but these are extremely difficult to keep for any length of time and they cannot be recommended for anyone except the highly skilled specialist. The average aquarist should decorate his tropical marine tank with the calcareous or horny skeletons of coral, after these have been thoroughly cleaned. In addition, some use what have been called 'living rocks', a term that will be explained below.

Coral reefs provide an intricate system of hiding-places for fishes and numerous invertebrates, and these require bright light and fast-moving water rich in oxygen. These factors obviously present some problems to anyone who is trying to establish some semblance of the natural habitat in an aquarium tank. In addition there is the problem of supplying an adequate and varied diet to many different kinds of fishes and invertebrates.

The basic food supply in the sea consists of the free-floating, mostly very small animals and plants known collectively as plankton. Planktonic plants include the diatoms, tiny green cells which float near the surface and provide food for many planktonic animals. Some of these animals are the larvae of animals living on the sea floor, whereas others are adults, albeit tiny ones.

Coral reef fishes show some amazing adaptations. Fishes in general cannot scratch themselves and thus free themselves of external parasites. There is, however, a small fish, the cleaner wrasse, which removes parasites from other fishes, which have been seen to open their mouths and spread their gill covers to allow the wrasse to pick off the parasites, which it then eats. There is also a prawn which acts as a cleaner.

The phenomenon of symbiosis, in which two quite different animals live together, is also widespread in coral reefs. There is, for instance, a close relationship between the clownfishes or anemone-fishes of the genus *Amphiprion* and certain large tropical sea-anemones, each deriving some benefit from the association.

When buying tropical marine fishes and

invertebrates, care should be taken to examine them very carefully with a lens. In particular, the body and fins must be free of white spots or films, and of inflamed areas, the eyes should not be protruding, and the swimming movements should be normal. Many newly imported fishes will not have fed for some time, and this lowers their resistance to disease. A concave belly often denotes hunger, and anal inflammation suggests a digestive disorder.

8 Tanks and equipment for the tropical marine aquarium

Angle-iron tanks of the type used for freshwater fishes are not suitable for marine animals, because sea water is highly corrosive. Nowadays most marine aquarists would buy an all-glass tank, in which the glass panes are cemented together with silicone rubber, which gives a practically indestructible joint; such tanks are, of course, non-corrosible. As an alternative it is possible to make a tank out of asbestos-cement sheets. In such a tank only the front is glass, and the other walls and the bottom should be carefully coated, when absolutely dry, with a good-quality epoxy resin. This not only reduces porosity, but it also prevents any possible toxins from leaching out of the cement.

Heaters for marine tanks should be enclosed in glass, with a plastic cap that is resistant to sea water. Lighting should present no special difficulties, as there are several types on the market.

All marine aquarium tanks will require some form of filtration, circulation and aeration. Filtration keeps the water optically clear, while circulation of the water and its aeration keep the water moving which is of prime importance for marine fishes and invertebrates. A submerged centrifugal pump will remove particles of detritus, draw in fresh air, and circulate the water satisfactorily.

Some marine aquarists recommend a foam filter or protein skimmer which is a piece of apparatus designed to remove some of the

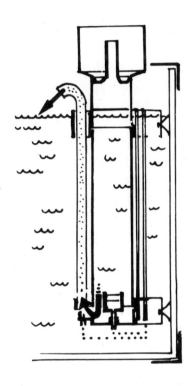

A protein skimmer helps to remove organic waste from the aquarium water

organic waste, mostly of an albuminous nature. The water is passed into a container where it is mixed with air. There it forms a foam which rises up into a detachable receiver at the top. The accumulated foam is discarded at intervals, thus removing much of the organic waste from the tank. Ozone (a form of oxygen with three linked oxygen atoms) can also be used in conjunction with a protein skimmer. The ozone, produced by an ozonizer, is mixed with the air

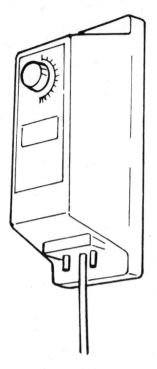

An ozonizer produces a mixture of ozone and air

which are encrusted with corals, dead and empty snail and bivalve shells, and disused calcareous worm tubes, bound together by calcareous algae, and producing a structure with numerous crevices and holes. On the reef itself such structures form the natural habitat for a rich fauna, consisting of sea-squirts, sponges, small tubeworms, free-living bristle-worms, small crustaceans and tiny brittlestars. On grounds of cost it would scarcely be feasible to import 'living rock' from tropical seas, but it is possible to find comparable pieces in subtropical areas, such as the Mediterranean Sea, in depths of 8–10 metres (approximately 25–30 feet). If any of these are used, care should be taken to remove any sponges, as these die quickly and pollute the water. Even if it contains no living animals, this type of calcareous material will keep the pH of the sea water constant, usually in the region of 8·0–8·3.

Pieces of dead coral can also be used in marine tanks, but they must be carefully cleaned, as they may well contain the remains of dead coral polyps. They should be soaked for some days in a 5–10% solution of sodium hydroxide (caustic

entering the protein skimmer, and this is said to increase the latter's efficiency.

Ultra-violet radiation can be used to kill bacteria, but it must be emphasized that certain bacteria perform an important function in the aquarium. In a well maintained tank the aerobic bacteria, requiring oxygen, break down organic waste substances into water, carbon dioxide and mineral salts, so it would be a mistake to kill them. On the other hand anaerobic bacteria (which work without oxygen) produce undesirable, evil-smelling products, but such bacteria should not be present in any numbers in a properly maintained tank. So it is inadvisable to use an ultra-violet lamp over a healthy tank.

Marine tanks cannot be decorated in the same way as a freshwater aquarium, in which the materials used, e.g. roots, peat, tend to lower the pH instead of keeping it stable. Marine tanks require a stable pH and this can be achieved by using calcareous materials, such as pieces of dead coral.

In recent years marine aquarists have been using what have come to be known as 'living rocks'. These are pieces of sedimentary rock

Before rocks are transported, any sponges should be removed from them, as they quickly die and foul the water

soda), care being taken to keep this dangerous material from any exposed parts of the body. They must then be thoroughly washed in running water.

The substrate is also important, and is often a decorative feature. Ordinary sea sand can be used as a substrate for the tank, but coral sand is even better. This comes from tropical beaches and it consists largely of coral fragments. The shell gravel found in temperate seas is comparable and consists mainly of broken mollusc shells. In tanks containing wrasses which bury themselves at night at least part of the substrate should be soft.

In general, seaweeds are very difficult to keep in a marine tank. There are, however, some green algae which grow well provided they are not eaten by fishes and sea-urchins. These include certain green algae belonging to the genus *Caulerpa*, the best known species being *C. prolifera*, but others can be used, e.g. *C. macrodisca*, *C. racemosa* and *C. sertularioides*. These small algae spread by means of creeping stolons and soon cover rocks and pieces of dead coral.

The microscopic algae known as diatoms

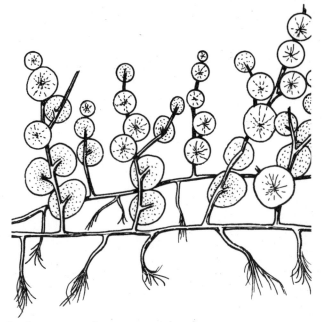

Caulerpa macrodisca, a green algae

grow if the water contains silicon compounds, which they use to make their external casing. They form a thin brown coating on rocks, but will disappear quickly if the silicon supply is exhausted. Green algae with long, filamentous fronds may also grow, but only if the fish population is fairly low, and the oxygen content of the water high.

Natural sea water can be used in a marine tank, but some aquarists prefer to make up an artificial sea water from a mixture of salts and trace elements. Salt mixtures in packs calculated for solution in different volumes of mains water are readily obtainable and easily dissolved.

When salts are dissolved to make artificial sea water, the whole solution should be left for several days, with a filter pump working, before the density is measured, using a hydrometer. The density reading will depend upon the temperature. The table on page 122, top, shows, for instance, that the density falls with increasing temperature.

On the average, tropical sea water at a temperature of 27°C (81°F) and with a density of about 1·023 will have a salinity (salt content) of 35 parts per thousand. In fact, the salinity of sea water is remarkably close to this figure in all

The green algae *Caulerpa prolifera* is the species that lives best in a marine aquarium

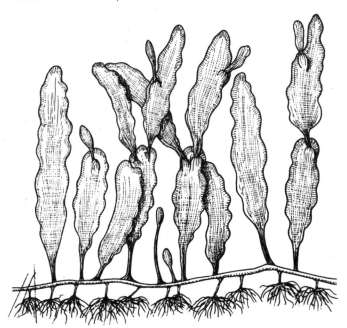

Relationship between temperature, salinity and density of sea water

Temperature in °C										
20	1·0193	1·0200	1·0208	1·0215	1·0223	1·0231	1·0239	1·0246	1·0253	1·0259
21	1·0191	1·0198	1·0206	1·0214	1·0221	1·0229	1·0237	1·0244	1·0251	1·0258
22	1·0189	1·0197	1·0204	1·0212	1·0219	1·0227	1·0235	1·0242	1·0249	1·0256
23	1·0187	1·0195	1·0202	1·0210	1·0217	1·0224	1·0232	1·0240	1·0248	1·0254
24	1·0184	1·0193	1·0200	1·0207	1·0215	1·0222	1·0230	1·0238	1·0245	1·0252
25	1·0182	1·0190	1·0197	1·0205	1·0213	1·0220	1·0228	1·0235	1·0242	1·0250
26	1·0179	1·0187	1·0194	1·0202	1·0210	1·0217	1·0224	1·0232	1·0239	1·0247
27	1·0175	1·0184	1·0191	1·0199	1·0206	1·0213	1·0221	1·0229	1·0237	1·0243
28	1·0172	1·0180	1·0188	1·0195	1·0203	1·0210	1·0218	1·0225	1·0233	1·0240
29	1·0169	1·0176	1·0184	1·0192	1·0200	1·0207	1·0214	1·0221	1·0229	1·0237
30	1·0165	1·0172	1·0180	1·0188	1·0195	1·0202	1·0210	1·0217	1·0225	1·0233
Salinity in parts per thousand	28	29	30	31	32	33	34	35	36	37

parts of the world, except in certain areas where there is dilution by fresh water.

The solution of salts can, therefore, be brought up to a concentration that will give a density of 1·023 and this will suit most tropical marine fishes and invertebrates. If the salinity does increase owing to evaporation, it is a simple matter to reduce it by adding fresh water.

At higher salinities the capacity of the water to dissolve oxygen decreases. The adjacent table shows how the oxygen saturation of the water depends upon temperature and density.

The pH of natural sea water is remarkably constant, at around 8·0–8·3, so it is slightly alkaline. The pH can be measured relatively simply, using a kit obtainable from dealers. This should be done at regular intervals, because in an aquarium tank the pH tends to fall, mainly because of the presence of dissolved carbonic acid. If the pH is found to be below 8·0 it can be adjusted by adding a small quantity of sodium bicarbonate.

A newly established marine tank should be allowed to rest for three or four weeks before any fishes are introduced. This will allow the pH to become stabilized and the aerobic bacteria to break down toxic substances in the water.

		Oxygen in cc per litre		
Temperature in °C	Density (approx.)	1·0225	1·0245	1·0255
10		6·54	6·46	6·37
15		5·94	5·87	5·80
20		5·44	5·38	5·31
25		4·99	4·94	4·85
30		4·56	4·50	4·44

9 Diet and diseases of tropical marine fishes

Feeding

In the sea tropical marine fishes feed throughout most of the day. It is not always possible for them to do this in the aquarium, but they should be given an adequate and varied diet. They will also eat the algae and small invertebrates in the tank.

Most marine fishes will eat the flesh of mussels or other bivalve molluscs, but it may be some time before they will accept food to which they are unaccustomed. Freeze-dried mysids, shrimps and prawns are easy to feed, and they have a high nutritive value. If they are used it should not be necessary to feed freshwater live foods, such as *Tubifex*, which die very rapidly in sea water, and if not consumed will soon decompose and cause pollution. Deep-frozen foods such as shrimps and prawns can also be used.

Coralfish diseases

It is likely that many marine fishes already carry infections when they are taken from the sea, but these may only become acute when there is an injury to the skin during capture or changes in oxygen saturation or temperature during transport. Unsuitable feeding and the presence of toxic substances are also factors that may affect the incidence of disease.

In general, diseases may be due to the presence of parasites, or to certain external factors.

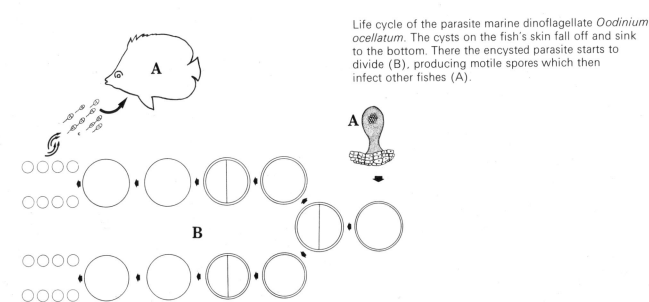

Life cycle of the parasite marine dinoflagellate *Oodinium ocellatum*. The cysts on the fish's skin fall off and sink to the bottom. There the encysted parasite starts to divide (B), producing motile spores which then infect other fishes (A).

Parasitic diseases are caused by organisms, such as protozoans (ciliates, flagellates, sporozoans), bacteria, viruses and fungi. The best known and most dangerous is caused by the dinoflagellate protozoan *Oodinium ocellatum*. These microscopic parasites infect and grow in the skin–(A) in the figure on page 123. They then fall to the bottom as cysts, which divide repeatedly, finally producing enormous numbers of free-swimming, flagellate dinospores (B). These attack new hosts and the cycle is repeated. In an aquarium tank, with much less water per fish than in the sea, the dinospores have no difficulty in finding and settling on a suitable host.

The rate of multiplication depends upon the temperature of the water. At a temperature of over 25°C (77°F), each cyst will have produced 256 dinospores in three days. At lower temperatures the rate of multiplication is much slower, and below 10°C (50°F) it ceases altogether. If the fishes are removed from an infected tank the cycle will go on until the dinospore stage is reached. Then the dinospores, finding no available host, will all die. In addition to high temperatures, a slightly alkaline pH (around 8·0), a high content of nitrate, and a water density of 1·012 to 1·021 also stimulate multiplication of the parasites.

Oodinium infections can be treated in various ways. Some authorities recommend the systematic transfer of the fishes through a series of tanks, the idea being to leave the parasites behind in tanks without fishes, so that they soon die off. Others recomend various drugs such as mepacrine derivatives, but these should only be used by experienced aquarists who have read the available literature on the subject.

One of the best methods of controlling *Oodinium* is to treat the water with a solution of copper sulphate as soon as symptoms of the disease have been observed; the dose should be at the rate of 163 milligrams of copper sulphate to 100 litres of tank water. First prepare a stock solution by dissolving 20 grams (approximately ¾oz) of copper sulphate in 5 litres (9 pints) of water; this should be kept in a well-stoppered plastic bottle. To use the chemical, add 25 cubic centimetres (millilitres), nearly 1 fluid oz, of the stock solution to every 100 litres (22 gallons) of aquarium water. The infected fishes can be left in this diluted copper solution for several days.

The copper sulphate causes the fish to shed the mucus covering the body, a rather drastic event, and so treatment with copper sulphate should only be carried out on fishes that show the thin coating of tiny white spots that is characteristic of *Oodinium*. The use of copper as a preventive measure on apparently healthy fishes is not recommended.

Oodinium first appears as tiny white spots or nodules on the skin and fins of the fish. These spread rapidly. The gills then become infected and the fish shows respiratory distress, remaining just below the water surface or close to a source of oxygen. If the infection has reached this stage it is scarcely possible to save the fish.

Oodinium infections can sometimes be prevented by reducing the content of nitrate in the water. This involves removing detritus and scraps of unconsumed food from the bottom, and also any decaying fragments of algae at the water surface. A high nitrate content can also be reduced by changing a proportion of the water at intervals.

The copper treatment should never be used in a tank containing invertebrates. The presence of this metal is lethal to such animals, and the rapid decomposition of their bodies will soon kill off the other inmates of the tank. Filamentous green algae are also adversely affected by copper. Certain fish species, such as the butterflyfishes of the family Chaetodontidae, do not tolerate a high dosage of copper, and in such cases the dosage recommended above should be reduced by 20–30%. If the tank is fitted with a foam filter, it should be turned off during the period of treatment; otherwise the drug will be removed from the tank water. On the other hand, there should be full aeration and water circulation.

Cryptocarion disease is caused by a ciliate

protozoan, *Cryptocarion irritans,* which settles as white nodules on the fins, skin and eyes and is very infectious. The nodules soon spread over the whole of the body, and inflamed areas of skin start to fall off. This disease can be treated in the same way as *Oodinium,* taking care that the treatment is not stopped before the last nodules have disappeared.

Fungal infections, often known as fin rot and mouth rot, appear as opaque coatings on the body and fins. They are due to various aquatic fungi, which are probably present in most natural waters but only become pathogenic and settle on fishes when environmental conditions change. Fishes from the Caribbean area are apparently more susceptible to fungal infection than those from other seas. In many cases of fungal infection a change of the tank water may help. If only the fins are attacked, the affected areas can be cut off, taking care not to damage the fin bases. In particularly serious cases the tank can be treated for some days with the fungicide griseofulvin at the rate of 25 milligrams per litre of water.

Lymphocystis is a less infectious disease caused by a virus which enters the cells of a fish and causes them to swell. It appears as pearly nodules of varying sizes, particularly on the back and the dorsal fins. The nodules usually appear first on the fins, and the infected areas can then be carefully cut off with a pair of fine scissors. The disease can often be cured by careful nursing, but in serious cases the fish can be given a copper sulphate bath (as for *Oodinium*) over a period, or they can be kept in a potassium iodide bath. Here the stock solution is made up by dissolving 5 grams (approximately $\frac{1}{8}$oz) of iodine and 500 grams (approximately 18oz) of potassium iodide in 5 litres (approximately 1·1 gallons) of distilled water. The dosage is the same as for copper, i.e. 25cc (nearly 1 fluid oz) of stock solution for each 100 litres (22 gallons) of tank water.

Swimbladder trouble is due to inflammation of the swimbladder, usually resulting from a drop in temperature during transport. The fish show jerky swimming movements usually with the head upwards. They should be put into a separate tank with a high water temperature (28–30°C or 82–86°F). The heat treatment can be reinforced by feeding on mussel flesh soaked in an antibiotic such as aureomycin.

10 Marine fishes

The selection of fish species for a marine tank must depend upon a number of factors, including coloration, size, fin shape and of course compatibility. Large forms such as triggerfishes must not be put into a tank with more delicate species which will have their fins nipped.

Invertebrates can, of course, occupy the same tank as fishes, but this needs care and experience. Obviously it would be unwise to put into a tank with invertebrates any fishes that will eat them. Such fishes include butterflyfishes, larger wrasse, parrotfishes, triggerfishes, boxfishes, porcupinefishes and pufferfishes. On the other hand, the smaller marine angelfishes and surgeonfishes, as well as various groupers, small gobies, blennies and scorpionfishes would be quite suitable. The association between sea-anemones and clown-fishes of the genus *Amphiprion* is only successful in an aquarium tank if the anemone is considerably larger than the fishes. The following pages give some details on a representative selection of marine fishes that are available.

Moray-eels (family Muraenidae)

Several species are suitable for the home aquarium, at any rate when they are young. These include the Blue ribbon eel *Rhinomuraena ambonensis*, a slender fish up to 120 cm (48 in) long with blue and yellow coloration, the Zebra moray *Echidna zebra* (up to 120 cm or 48 in), the Snowflake moray *E.*

nebulosa (80 cm or 32 in) and the voracious Leopard moray *Gymnothorax favagineus* (= *G. tesselata*) (150cm or 60in). Moray-eels become active as soon as it starts to get dark, and they should be kept in a spacious tank, but not with smaller fishes. The tank should have a close-fitting lid. They can be fed chopped fish and squid, as well as mussel flesh.

Many moray-eels live in shallow water, often among rocks, where they prey on octopus, which they seize with their sharp-pointed teeth. A moray cannot cut the prey into pieces with these teeth. Instead they have been observed to twist their body round very rapidly on its own axis so that the prey is broken into pieces.

Plotosus lineatus, a marine catfish

Marine catfishes (family Plotosidae)

There are several species in the Indian Ocean and off northern Australia. They are nocturnal, and great care must be taken in handling them, as the dorsal and pectoral fins have poison spines. Like their relatives in fresh water, these catfishes are often useful as scavengers. They

Adioryx diadema, striped squirrelfish

are best bought when quite young, and kept in a small shoal.

The species usually kept is *Plotosus lineatus*, which grows to a length of 70 cm (27 in), and has an elongated, torpedo-like body and a large head, with four pairs of short barbels. The first dorsal fin is normal, but the second dorsal fin is combined with the caudal and anal fins to form a single fringe. These catfishes can be kept in sea or brackish water, at a temperature of 22—26°C (72–79°F).

Anglerfishes
(family Antennariidae)

These fishes have an 'angle' or lure, a modified first dorsal fin ray positioned between the mouth and eyes, which has a flap of skin at the end. The larger species are unsuitable for the home aquarium, but small species such as the Sargassum fish *Histrio histrio* are worth having. It grows to a length of 15 cm (6 in). In nature this species feeds exclusively on live food.

Soldierfishes
(family Holocentridae)

Soldierfishes are crepuscular and nocturnal and they normally do well in captivity, once acclimatized. They are not active swimmers and spend the day hidden in rock crevices. Suitable species for the aquarium include *Holocentrus xantherythrus* (25 cm or $9\frac{3}{4}$ in), the Striped squirrelfish *Adioryx diadema* and a few species of *Myripristis*, e.g. the bigeye squirrelfish *M. murdjan* (30 cm or $11\frac{3}{4}$ in).

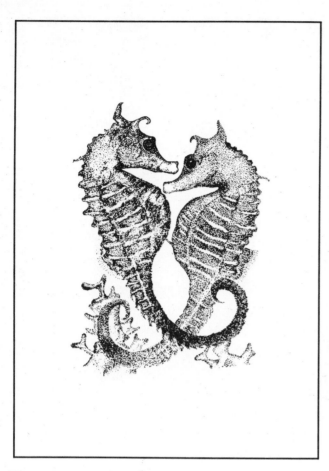

Hippocampus, a sea-horse. A female (right) transferring eggs into the male's brood pouch where the young fishes will develop

Sea-horses and pipefishes (family Syngnathidae)

Sea-horses cling to seaweed, and only rarely swim after food, preferring to wait until it passes close to them. Pipefishes, on the other hand, have a long slender body and are more active and therefore relatively easier to feed. Both sea-horses and pipefishes should be kept in a species tank without other fishes which tend to compete for the available food.

The female sea-horse lays her eggs in a brood pouch on the belly of the male, who carries them around until they hatch into miniatures of their parents. Commonly imported sea-horses include *Hippocampus kuda* (15 cm or 6 in) from south-east Asia, the Northern sea-horse *H. hudsonius* (20 cm or 7¾ in) from the western tropical Atlantic and *H. zosterae* (5 cm or 2 in) from the West Indies. Sea-horses and pipefishes

feed naturally on small live food, such as plankton, but they will also eat very young guppies and other livebearers.

Pterois volitans, scorpion fish

Scorpionfishes (family Scorpaenidae)

These fishes are voracious predators, with highly venomous dorsal and pectoral fin rays, which approach their prey and when close enough they open their very large mouth and swallow the prey whole. They can be accustomed to taking pieces of fish, but they prefer live fishes. The genus *Pterois* contains the dragonfishes, also known as lionfishes and turkeyfishes. The species usually kept include *P. volitans*, *P. radiata*, *P. lunulata* and *P. antennata* which reach lengths of up to 25 cm (approximately 10 in).

Stonefishes (family Synanceiidae)

These are unattractive fishes with extremely venomous dorsal and pectoral fin rays. They lie on the bottom and are so well camouflaged that they look like stones covered with a growth of algae. They should be kept in a species tank and will eat almost anything, particularly other

Synanceja verrucosa, stonefish

fishes. Two species occasionally imported are *Synanceja verrucosa* and *S. horrida*.

Groupers (family Serranidae)

These are active predators which hide in caves or under rock ledges, and dash out to seize passing prey, a task for which the large mouth is well adapted. Smaller specimens can be kept for quite a time, and fed on pieces of chopped fish or squid.

The species imported include the black grouper *Epinephelus (Cephalopholis) argus* (38 cm or 15 in) and *E. (C.) miniatus* (46 cm or 18 in).

The six-lined grouper *Grammistes sexlineatus* (25 cm or 9¾ in) from the Indo-Pacific is a voracious fish that should only be kept with others that are considerably larger than itself.

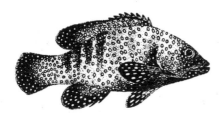

Epinephelus (Cephalopholis) argus, black grouper

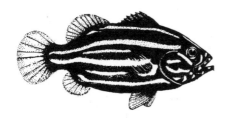

Grammistes sexlineatus, six-lined grouper

The family Grammidae

These are non-predatory fishes from the coral reefs of the Caribbean Sea and Bermuda. The royal gramma *(Gramma loreto)*, up to 6–8 cm (2¼–3 in), is sometimes kept, but it does not always settle down well.

Cardinal fishes (family Apogonidae)

These are nocturnal or crepuscular fishes, usually coloured reddish, which have two dorsal fins. They grow to a length of about 10 cm (3¾ in). Some, if not all, are known to be mouthbrooders, and in most cases it is apparently the male who incubates the eggs in his mouth.

The pyjama cardinal fish *Sphaeramia nematoptera* (8 cm or 3 in) must be kept in a small shoal, as solitary specimens do not survive. The shoal will remain more or less inactive during the day, but start to move around as soon as the light fades.

Sphaeramia nematoptera, pyjama cardinal fish

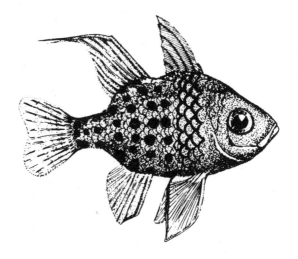

Snappers (family Lutjanidae)

Snappers are highly esteemed as edible fishes in the tropics and subtropics. They are predatory and grow rapidly so they soon become too large for the home aquarium. Species imported include the blue-striped snapper *Lutjanus kasmira* (38 cm or 15 in) and particularly *L.*

Gramma loreto, royal gramma

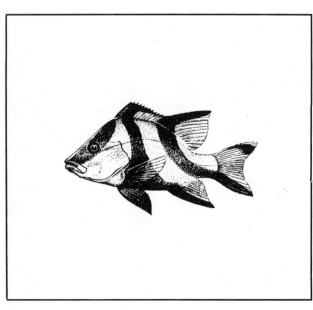

Lutjanus sebae, a snapper

Gaterin (= Plectorinchus) orientalis, oriental sweetlips
above: juvenile pattern
below: adult pattern

Sweetlips (family Pomadasyidae)

These fishes live and feed mainly on the bottom, and the young are more attractive than the adults. The species commonly kept is the oriental sweetlips *Gaterin (= Plectorinchus) orientalis*.

Fingerfishes (family Monodactylidae)

When young these fishes occur in fresh and brackish waters, but most move into the sea as

sebae, about the same size, which is brightly coloured when young, becoming much duller with age.

Monodactylus argenteus, mono or fingerfish

they grow older. The species available are *Monodactylus argenteus*, the mono or fingerfish (23 cm or 9 in) from the Indian Ocean, and *M. sebae* (20 cm or 7¾ in), a rather taller species from the west coast of Africa. They feed well in the aquarium, and as they get older they should be transferred to sea water and kept only in that.

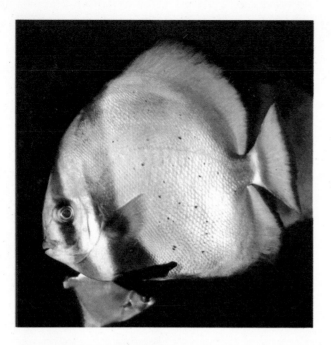

Platax orbicularis, a batfish

Batfishes (family Ephippidae)

These handsome fishes come from coastal waters in the Indo-Pacific region. They are sometimes difficult to acclimatize. The species available on the market are *Platax orbicularis* and *P. teira*, which under good conditions may grow to a length of 50–60 cm (20–23 in) and the rather smaller *P. pinnatus*.

Butterflyfishes (family Chaetodontidae)

A large family with numerous species which live in and around tropical coral reefs. Most are about 15–20 cm (16–18 in) long. They search for food, mainly small invertebrates, in the crevices in the corals. Butterflyfishes should not be kept with invertebrates such as prawns, as they tend

Chaetodon semilarvatus, a butterflyfish

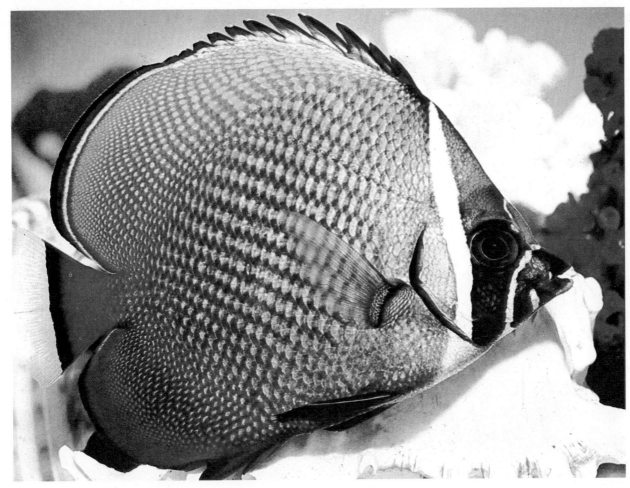

Chaetodon collaris, a butterflyfish

left: *Chaetodon tinkeri*, a butterflyfish
right: *Centropyge bicolor*

Chaetodon quadrimaculatus, a butterflyfish

to bite pieces off their long appendages. They are often aggressive towards members of their own species, but not usually towards other species. They are very susceptible to *Oodinium* infections, and unfortunately they do not

133

tolerate the usual copper sulphate treatment very well.

Several species are imported, including *Chaetodon collaris, C. semilarvatus, C. auriga, C. citrinellus, C. fremblii* and *C. ocellatus*. The more recently introduced *C. quadrimaculatus* and *C. tinkeri* are still expensive. Species with long snouts, such as *Chelmon rostratus* and *Forcipiger flavissimus,* are well adapted for extracting food from narrow crevices in the corals.

Pygoplites diacanthus, royal empress angelfish

Juvenile patterns of:
Pomacanthus semicirculatus, an angelfish
Pomacanthus imperator, imperial angelfish
Pomacanthus annularis, blue king angelfish

Marine angelfishes (family Pomacanthidae)

The members of this family are all brilliantly coloured, and it is interesting that in most of the species the coloration and pattern of the juvenile fishes are quite different from those of the adults. Adults of a species often fight with one another, and it is probable that the possession of a completely different pattern and colour will protect the young from the attacks of their elders. Most species are imported with a juvenile pattern, often of blue and white stripes, but even at this stage the different species can be recognized by certain distinctive features in the pattern.

Marine angelfishes can be fed on chopped fish or squid, but they must have some plant food, such as lettuce, unless the tank has a sufficient growth of algae.

The species from the Indo-Pacific include the Royal empress angelfish *Pygoplites diacanthus* (20 cm or $7\frac{3}{4}$ in), one of the most attractive of all coral fishes, but only suitable for the advanced marine aquarist. The Caribbean area has the queen angelfish *Holacanthus ciliaris* (60 cm or 24 in) and the blue angelfish *H. isabelita* (46 cm or 18 in), but these are not often seen on the market. The species more commonly imported include *Pomacanthus paru* and *P. arcuatus,* which usually settle down well in the aquarium and grow rapidly to about 40 cm ($15\frac{3}{4}$ in). The smaller rock beauty *Holacanthus tricolor* (30 cm or 12 in) and the cherubfish *Centropyge argi* (6 cm or $2\frac{1}{4}$ in) are also imported.

Some of the smaller marine angelfishes, such as the black-banded angelfish *Holacanthus arcuatus* (18 cm or 7 in) and the very attractive

Holacanthus ciliaris, queen angelfish;
right: a juvenile showing vertical bars

Holacanthus arcuatus, black-banded angelfish

Centropyge loriculus, come from the Hawaiian Islands, but the main area for pomacanthids is the Indo-Pacific (Red Sea and East Africa to the East Indies, Queensland, Fiji and many island groups of the South Pacific). Some of the species, such as *Pygoplites diacanthus* (20 cm or 7¾ in), the imperial angelfish *Pomacanthus imperator* (36 cm or 14 in), *P. semicirculatus* (40 cm or 15¾ in) and *Arusetta asfur* (14 cm or 5½ in), grow quite large. Other species from the Indo-Pacific are the Blue king angelfish *Pomacanthus annularis* (40 cm or 15¾ in), the blue-girdled angelfish, *Euxiphippos navarchus* (30 cm or

Arusetta asfur, a marine angelfish

Abudefduf oxyodon, a damselfish

Damselfishes and anemone-fishes (family Pomacentridae)

Most of these fishes live in shoals among coral, in some cases in close association with sea-anemones. Although quite small they are often aggressive towards one another.

The damselfishes include *Abudefduf oxyodon* (11 cm or $4\frac{1}{4}$ in), *A. xanthurus*, and the larger sergeant-major *A. saxatilis*. In the genus *Dascyllus*, the domino damselfish *D. trima-culatus* (12 cm or $4\frac{3}{4}$ in) is commonly imported. Other members of this genus include *D. aruanus* (9 cm or $3\frac{1}{2}$ in) and *D. reticulatus* (7 cm or $2\frac{3}{4}$ in).

Anemone-fishes all come from the Indo-Pacific where they live in close association with certain large tropical sea-anemones, swimming in and out of the tentacles; a behaviour pattern that would be fatal to other fishes. Most of them belong to the genus *Amphiprion*. They can be kept together with their anemone in a marine tank, but it is advisable for the latter to be large in relation to the size of the anemone-fishes.

The naming of *Amphiprion* species is a somewhat confused subject, partly because some species resemble each other very closely when young, and partly because their colours change with age.

Suitable species include the common

Euxiphipops xanthometopon, yellow-faced angelfish

$11\frac{3}{4}$ in), the six-barred angelfish *E. sexstriatus* and the yellow-faced angelfish *E. xanthome-topon* (30 cm or $11\frac{3}{4}$ in). Although these are all highly attractive fishes many are still difficult to keep for any length of time, except in the hands of really experienced aquarists.

Amphiprion sebae, an anemone-fish

Abudefduf xanthurus, a damselfish

Cleaner wrasse, *Labroides dimidiatus*

False cleaner, *Aspidontus taeniatus*

Another cleaner wrasse, *Labroides quadrilineatus*, from the Red Sea

Dascyllus aruanus, a damselfish

anemone-fish or clownfish *Amphiprion ocellaris* (10 cm or 3¾ in), formerly known as *A. percula*, *A. sebae*, *A. polymnus* (12 cm or 4¾ in) and *A. ephippium* (15 cm or 6 in).

Wrasses (family Labridae)

A large family with numerous species in tropical and subtropical waters, and also some in temperate waters. They are popular aquarium fishes which feed on almost any food, live or

dead, and do not appear to be too demanding as regards the quality of the water.

The cleaner wrasse *Labroides dimidiatus* (10 cm or 3¾ in) is of particular interest on account of its habit of removing parasites and loose fragments of skin from other fishes, a task which the latter obviously encourage, and they never attack the wrasse. The quite unrelated False cleaner *Aspidontus taeniatus*, a blenny, has a behaviour pattern very similar to that of the Cleaner wrasse, but it is an aggressive fish that bites the fins of other species.

Some wrasses change their coloration as they grow older. This happens, for instance, in *Coris gaimardi* (= *formosa*), from the Indo-Pacific, in which the young are red with a white pattern, but adults are completely different in colour (see illustrations).

Blennies (family Blenniidae)

A widespread family of small fishes with a blunt head, with numerous species in tropical, subtropical and temperate seas. Species imported from tropical waters include the forktail blenny, *Meiacanthus atrodorsalis* and the yellow-tailed blenny *M. mossambicus*. Some of the subtropical species, such as *Blennius pavo* (12 cm or 4¾ in) and *B. sphinx* (8 cm or 3 in), both from the Mediterranean Sea, have proved very hardy, if somewhat quarrelsome, aquarium fishes.

Coris gaimardi, a wrasse, with a juvenile (right) for comparison

Dragonets (family Callionymidae)

This family includes the common dragonet *Callionymus lyra* of European waters which is sometimes seen in the temperate marine aquarium, but in recent years a tropical representative has appeared on the market. This is the mandarin fish *Synchiropus splendidus* from Indonesian waters, which grows to about 12 cm ($4\frac{3}{4}$ in). The sexes are easy to distinguish, for in the male the front rays of the first dorsal fin are much elongated. They feed primarily on the small invertebrates that live among the algae, taking them with the slightly protrusible mouth. They cannot really be kept for any length of time on a diet of *Tubifex* and *Artemia*. They should be kept in a large tank to prevent the males from fighting.

Gobies (family Gobiidae)

A very large family with at least 600 species, of mainly small fishes, some of which do well in the aquarium. Newly introduced gobies may hide away in a corner of the tank, but they gradually start to come out. They will eat almost anything, and since they have a large mouth can take relatively large morsels.

The best known species for a tropical tank are the neon goby *Gobiosoma oceanops* (6 cm or $2\frac{1}{4}$ in), from the Caribbean area, the slightly smaller *Gobiodon citrinus* from the Indo-Pacific and Red Sea, and the larger scissor-tail goby *Ptereleotris tricolor* (14 cm or $5\frac{1}{2}$ in) also from the Indo-Pacific area.

Surgeonfishes (family Acanthuridae)

The popular name refers to the small sharp spine on each side of the tail base, which is movable and can be folded back or erected so that it stands out at right angles to the body. In the latter position it forms a dangerous weapon for attack or defence. Surgeonfishes use this spine when fighting members of their own species or other fishes that threaten them, so some aquarists prefer to keep a single surgeon-fish alone in a tank, to avoid bloodshed.

Synchiropus splendidus, mandarin fish

Zebrasoma flavescens, yellow tang

Numerous species appear on the market, and these include the white-breasted surgeonfish *Acanthurus leucosternon* (30 cm or 12 in) from the Indian Ocean, the smaller golden-rimmed surgeon fish *A. glaucopareius* from the Philippines, and the clown surgeon *A. lineatus* (18 cm or 7 in) from the Indo-Pacific area. Another good species from the same area is the blue surgeon *Paracanthurus hepatus* (30 cm or 12 in). The genus *Zebrasoma* has several rather aggressive species including the sailfin tang *Z. veliferum* (40 cm or 15¾ in) from the Indo-Pacific, and the more peaceful yellow tang *Z.*

Acanthurus leucosternon, white-breasted surgeonfish

Paracanthurus hepatus, blue surgeonfish

Zanclus canescens, a Moorish idol fish

flavescens from the Hawaiian area. The form known as *Z. desjardini* is very similar in external appearance to *Z. veliferum*, but its tail is marked with numerous spots which are lacking in the latter species.

Moorish idols (family Zanclidae)

A small group of rather strange, quite small fishes which require a large tank with a volume of at least 350 litres (approximately 75 gallons), and plenty of plant food, so a good growth of algae in the tank will be an advantage. There are several varieties based on small differences in pattern, but these are now all classified as *Zanclus canescens* (20 cm or $7\frac{3}{4}$ in).

Pseudobalistes fuscus, blue-lined triggerfish

Triggerfishes (family Balistidae)

Strangely shaped fishes, often beautifully coloured, with a very large head and a small mouth
with powerful teeth. The first dorsal fin ray is in
the form of a large spine which can be erected
and locked into position by the second shorter
spiny ray, forming a trigger mechanism. The
erectile spine serves as a weapon and also helps
to anchor or wedge the fishes in rocky crevices
during the night. Triggerfishes are best kept
separate in the aquarium, as they are usually
aggressive, except when young.

Balistoides niger, clown triggerfish

In the sea triggerfishes feed mainly on marine invertebrates, such as crustaceans, sea-urchins and bivalve molluscs, and so can be given mussel flesh in the aquarium. Large individuals will eat lean heart or liver, chopped into small pieces.

Lactoria cornuta, long-horned cowfish

Rhinecanthus aculeatus, Picasso triggerfish

Suitable species for the aquarium include the undulate triggerfish *Balistapus undulatus* (30 cm or 12), the clown triggerfish *Balistoides niger* (50 cm or 19½ in), the black triggerfish *Odonus niger* (50 cm or 19½ in), the similarly sized blue-lined triggerfish *Pseudobalistes fuscus*, all from the Indo-Pacific area, and the very bizarre Picasso triggerfish *Rhinecanthus aculeatus* (33 cm or 13 in) from Hawaii.

Boxfishes (family Ostraciontidae)

These are angular fishes with the body enclosed in bony plates, except for the fins. The tail fin with its very flexible peduncle acts as a rudder. The powerful teeth are well adapted for crushing hard-shelled animals, particularly crustaceans.

Boxfishes are not easy to keep in the aquarium and they often do not survive the period of acclimatization. It is advisable to keep several individuals (even of different species) together, as they appear to learn from each other to take the substitute foods offered by the aquarist. Dying boxfishes produce a poisonous substance which may kill other perfectly healthy fishes.

Imported species include the long-horned cowfish *Lactoria cornuta* (50 cm or 19½ in), the spotted boxfish *Ostracion meleagris* (= *lentiginosum*) (20 cm or 7¾ in), and the thornback boxfish *Tetrosomus gibbosus* (30 cm or 12 in), all from the Indo-Pacific.

Pufferfishes (family Tetraodontidae)

A family with numerous representatives in all tropical and subtropical seas, and a few in fresh and brackish waters. Pufferfishes are so called from their ability to inflate the body. Their flesh which is eaten in Japan, for instance, is often poisonous. The powerful beak is well adapted for crushing hard-shelled invertebrates. They sometimes blow away the sand with a jet of water, and thus expose crustaceans and other suitable prey. In an aquarium they can be fed on chopped mussel or fish flesh, but they should not be kept in a tank with invertebrates, which they will soon eat.

Canthigaster valentini, a pufferfish

Suitable species for the aquarium include *Arothron nigropunctatus* (25 cm or 9¾ in) from the Indo-Pacific area, but the smaller species with pointed heads are perhaps more suitable for the home aquarium. They include *Canthigaster margaritatus* (15 cm or 6 in) and the related *C. valentini* (20 cm or 7¾ in), both from the Indo-Pacific.

Diodon hystrix, a porcupinefish

Porcupinefishes (family Diodontidae)

These fishes are also able to inflate themselves. The mouth is again small, but the bite powerful. The protruding eyes can be turned in all directions, thus giving the fish a very wide visual field. On coral reefs these fishes often live in association with soldierfishes. Species frequently kept include *Diodon holacanthus* (50 cm or 19½ in) and *D. hystrix* (86 cm or 35 in), both from tropical seas, but these are only suitable for the home aquarium when young.

11 Invertebrates for the marine aquarium

Unlike the vertebrates (fishes, amphibians, reptiles, birds and mammals), the invertebrates comprise all those animals which do not have a vertebral column. Some invertebrates do, however, have an external hard skeleton or shell, e.g. crustaceans, snails, bivalves, sea-urchins.

The principal marine invertebrates are the coelenterates (sea anemones, jellyfishes, corals), the sponges, the molluscs (gastropods or snails, bivalves and octopuses), the worms (bristle-worms, tubeworms) and the echinoderms (starfishes, brittlestars, sea-urchins, sea-cucumbers, feather-stars). Many of these can be kept in the aquarium but some are not easy to maintain. They are considerably more sensitive to the quality of the water than the true fishes.

Sponges
A sponge consists of numerous microscopic cells which take in sea water and filter minute food particles from it. Suitable food of this type is not usually present in an aquarium, so sponges are not to be recommended except for the very experienced. They should be placed in a dimly lit corner of the tank, as they will soon die if algae start to grow on their surface.

Coelenterates
The body of a coelenterate is a hollow sac open at the top end where the mouth is surrounded by rings of tentacles. Prey is caught by sting cells

An orange-red sponge

on the tentacles and passed into the mouth, and thence into the hollow sac where it is digested. Jellyfishes are not suitable for the aquarium, but various kinds of sea-anemones can be kept successfully, and occasionally small pieces of live coral.

Sea-anemones are found in all tropical and subtropical seas, and also on the shores in temperate regions. Most of those kept in the marine aquarium come from tropical waters where some of them grow to over three feet in diameter. For the home aquarium they would need to be much smaller than this.

The association of anemone-fishes (genus

Amphiprion) with large sea-anemones has already been mentioned. Under aquarium conditions it seems that the anemones usually get the worst of the bargain. They require a plentiful supply of oxygen and a fast water circulation. They should not, however, be put immediately in front of the water inlet, but should be sheltered from the direct current by rocks.

The sea-anemones of the order *Cerianthana* live with the body buried in the sand or gravel.

They emerge and unfold their delicate tentacles when conditions in the tank are to their liking, but will immediately withdraw and become invisible if disturbed. They can be fed on small pieces of mussel-flesh or freeze-dried prawns dropped onto the crown of tentacles.

The anemones that live in association with anemone-fishes mostly belong to the genera *Stoichactis* and *Discosoma*, but these are primarily plankton-feeders, so they rarely get enough food in the aquarium and gradually

A sea-anemone *(Radianthus)* with a symbiotic prawn *(Periclimenes)*

become smaller and smaller, and finally die. The related genus *Radianthus* has some species which appear to do better in captivity, particularly the Caribbean one, known in the trade as the Florida anemone. These anemones will accept the presence of the fishes even though there are no anemone-fishes in their home waters (all species of *Amphiprion* and related genera are restricted to the Indo-Pacific).

Gorgonians

The gorgonians are colonial coelenterates that live in areas where brisk currents bring them the plankton on which they feed. Live gorgonians can be kept in a marine tank, provided the water circulation is really efficient and as long as algae are not allowed to grow on them. Their horny skeletons are very decorative.

Molluscs

The phylum Mollusca is one of the major groups of the animal kingdom. The most important classes are the gastropods (snails, slugs), the bivalves (mussels, oysters, clams) and the cephalopods (squids, cuttlefishes and octopuses). Many gastropods and bivalves are imported from tropical seas and some live quite well in marine tanks. Among the gastropods there are several very attractive cowries, such as the tiger cowry *Cypraea tigris* and the related *C. mappa* and *C. mauritiana*. Only small specimens should be kept, and in a well-established tank they will find their own food, browsing algae from the rocks and picking up scraps of food left by other animals. The genus *Murex* also has species that do well, although they are mainly active at night. These are, however, predators, and they will attack and eat other animals such as worms and sea-urchins. Another gastropod sometimes imported is *Mitra papalis*.

Cone shells are sometimes sold, but they are extremely dangerous animals to have in a tank. They produce a venom which they inject into their prey. A small fish attacked by a cone shell dies immediately.

Bivalve molluscs have two valves of the shell

A cowry *(Cypraea* species) showing (top) the shell completely covered by the mantle and (bottom) the shell partially exposed by the withdrawal of the mantle

joined by a hinge, and they can be closed by the contraction of a powerful muscle. Bivalves in which this muscle is not functioning should not be bought, as they will certainly die in quite a short time and the decay of their soft parts will pollute the water. Species imported include *Lima scabra* and small specimens of *Tridacna*, but these are plankton feeders and can take only very small particles. *Tridacna* species have algal cells (zooxanthellae) living in their tissues. These cells need light, and in nature they receive plenty because the clams always live in shallow water. In the aquarium they should be placed so as to receive the maximum amount of light. Even so they do not usually survive for long in the home aquarium.

A group of corals and small tubeworms

Worms

The phylum Annelida includes the earthworms and leeches, which do not concern us here, and also the bristle-worms or Polychaeta, some of which are very attractive in a marine tank, particularly those that live in tubes of their own making. Such tubeworms, belonging to the families Serpulidae, Sabellidae and Terebellidae, are usually imported attached to pieces of rock, which may also house other sessile animals, such as corals and sponges. Some tubeworms construct their tube out of sand particles cemented by a slimy secretion; others make a calcareous tube. The worms living in these tubes expand their tentacles to catch food particles, but if disturbed they can withdraw the whole crown of tentacles in a fraction of a second. Most tanks will have enough suspended particles to feed a few tubeworms.

Crustaceans

Crustaceans range in size from tiny water-fleas to giant crabs. Some live on land, but most are aquatic. Several crustaceans of the group Decapoda can be kept in the aquarium. Larger decapods such as lobsters and crawfishes are only suitable for a public aquarium, but many of the smaller shrimps and prawns do very well in the home aquarium. One of the best is *Stenopus hispidus*, which has an attractive pattern and has been seen to clean scraps of skin from fishes. This species can be kept as a true pair, but two of the same sex will quarrel. Such small crustaceans will live perfectly well on the scraps left by the fishes.

Some prawns live in association with sea-anemones, a phenomenon known as symbiosis. Two species that live in this way are *Periclimenes brevicarpalis* and *P. pedersoni*. On the other hand the little harlequin prawn, *Hymenocera picta*, has very different habits, for it feeds mainly on starfishes. Often working with a partner of the same species, it is able to turn over a starfish and then gradually eat it.

Hermit-crabs are decapod crustaceans that live with the soft, rear part of their body tucked into an empty gastropod shell. As they grow they have to change their shell for a larger size, so a tank containing hermit-crabs should have a

The predatory prawn *Hymenocera picta*, eating a starfish, *Protoreaster lincki*

Cleaner prawn, *Stenopus hispidus*

selection of empty shells of various sizes. Hermit-crabs are predatory and so quite unsuitable for a tank containing invertebrates. The red hermit-crab, *Dardanus megistos,* is an attractive species often imported.

Some of the small crabs imported from tropical shores are also suitable for the aquarium. Many of these spend part of their time out of the water, and they can therefore be kept in a tank with shallow water, with a few rocks sticking up out of the water and a tiny beach of sand or gravel where the crabs can come out at will. Among these are the well-known fiddler-crabs of the genus *Uca* in which the male has a particularly large pincer on one side.

Echinoderms

These are exclusively marine animals forming the phylum Echinodermata. Starfishes do quite well provided they have not suffered injury during collection and transit. They move about with the help of hydraulically operated tubefeet, each of which has a small sucker at the end. These enable them to climb vertical surfaces underwater. Most starfishes are predatory, those with broad arms, such as *Oreaster*, *Pentaceraster* and *Protoreaster* usually being more active predators than those with round arms, such as the blue starfish *Linckia laevigata,* and species of *Echinaster* and *Ophidiaster*. *Linckia* is probably the most suitable tropical starfish for an aquarium tank.

Sea-urchins are rather more sensitive to the quality of the water, and they also require a supply of algae. In a sea-urchin not in healthy condition the spines will droop, whereas in a healthy specimen they are held erect. If the spines are shed the sea-urchin is more or less moribund, and should be immediately removed from the tank. Sea-urchins with very long spines are not often imported. The spines are very brittle, and in many species they carry poison at the tips, so great care must be taken when handling them. The small, oval sea-urchins of the genus *Echinometra* live quite well in the aquarium. The usual species imported are *Echinometra mathaei* (reddish-violet) from the Indo-Pacific and *E. lucunter* (pale grey).

Orange and blue sponges with a red sea-urchin

Acknowledgments

The publishers wish to thank the following for permission to use photographs and diagrams: Librairie Larousse for photographs on pages 9, 10, 15 (top), 18, 25 (top), 32 (bottom), 40, 48 (top right), 49 (left), 52 (top) 53 (top), 62 (right), 63 (bottom), 65 (bottom), 66 (top right), 67 (left), 69 (top), 71 (top), 73, 77 (bottom), 78 (top), 81 (top), 85, 87 (bottom), 92 (bottom), 98 (top), 99 (top right), 100 (top), 110 (bottom), 111 (top), 113 (top); Hans Mayland for diagrams and all other photographs.

General index

Index of plants

Index of fishes and invertebrates

Index of diseases